This is How We See the World

This is How We See the World

John B. Lee

First Edition

Hidden Brook Press
www.HiddenBrookPress.com
writers@HiddenBrookPress.com

Copyright © 2017 Hidden Brook Press
Copyright © 2017 John B. Lee

All rights for poems and all written content reverts to the author. All rights for book, layout and design remain with Hidden Brook Press. No part of this book may be reproduced except by a reviewer who may quote brief passages in a review. The use of any part of this publication reproduced, transmitted in any form or by any means, electronic, mechanical, photocopied, recorded or otherwise stored in a retrieval system without prior written consent of the publisher is an infringement of the copyright law.

This is How We See the World
John B. Lee

Cover Design – Richard M. Grove
Layout and Design – Richard M. Grove

Typeset in Garamond
Printed and bound in Canada
Distributed in USA by Ingram,
       in Canada by Hidden Brook Distribution

Library and Archives Canada Cataloguing in Publication

Lee, John B., 1951-, author
    This is how we see the world / John B. Lee. -- First edition.

Poems with some prose.
ISBN 978-1-927725-50-4 (softcover)

    I. Title.

PS8573.E348T45 2017   C811'.54   C2017-905924-6

Thanks Tai for tweaking the author photo and for taking the photo on the back cover of this book. "Burnt by the Sun" ... indeed you have brought out the detail in this photo which is a *selfie* taken outside the ruins of the Lee Plaza Hotel in Detroit City. The Lee Plaza is where my mom and dad stayed on their honeymoon on January 8 and 9th 1949. It is now designated a heritage site. I took the photo late in the summer of 2016 when I did a poetry reading in Detroit City. I've read in America a number of times, but never before in Detroit – my old stompin' grounds. When I was a schoolboy we went there as a family crossing the border to Detroit every Labour Day to buy our school supplies. Detroit was the town where I bought all my Beatle records, and my first, last and only pair of Beatle Boots, complete with winkle picker toes, stretchy side panels, and Cuban heels thus elevating my grade nine 4 foot 10 pipsqueak body making me loom large in the halls of learning at Ridgetown District High School in September 1965.

This photo captures me recalling my mom when I was a mere embryo, my youth just as I was writing my very first poems post-Beatle February 64, and myself as a traveler through time in time come full circle in the closing lines of the first published poem written as a sixteen year old *"with nothing to do but to begin at the end."* The photo on the back is of me looking over the lake in a contemporary contemplation – here is where I am now.

to Cathy as always

and

to the dedicated publishers

of chapbooks who have featured

my work over the years

Table of Content

Forward by Roger Bell – *page 1*

Preface – Je Suis Désolé, Lo Siento, I'm Sorry – *page 7*

Poem for One or More Feet
… how to read this poem — *page 23*
prologue — *page 24*
Poem for One or More Feet — *page 25*
Why a Foot Should Be a Poem — *page 27*
Inspiration — *page 28*
… imagine yourself — *page 29*
Voices that Feet Have — *page 31*
The Uncloven Foot — *page 31*
Phasing — *page 32*
A Foot for all Seasons — *page 33*
The Path Taken — *page 34*
Feetish Journals — *page 36*
Remarks — *page 37*
Loving Feet — *page 37*
Fetus — *page 39*
Requiem for Feet Lost in Battle — *page 40*
The Knife — *page 41*
Inscription Found on an Instep — *page 42*
Portrait of the Artist as a Young Foot — *page 43*
Facts You Should Know about Feet i – xi — *page 45*

To Kill a White Dog – *page 49*

The Day Jane Fonda Came to Guelph
When the Old Poet Shambles Past — *page 62*
The Subtleties, Lunenburg, Nova Scotia — *page 63*
Riding with Dick — *page 64*
This Poem for Nothing – Ninety-two Second Bout — *page 66*

Spring — *page 67*
The Makers and the Spoilers — *page 68*
The Sequence — *page 71*
The Day Jane Fonda Came to Guelph — *page 73*
Joggers — *page 74*
A Heavy Harmless Sorrow — *page 76*
Soundless Voices — *page 78*
Spreading Vetch — *page 79*
When You are Gone Away — *page 80*
I Wake to Breathe Your Beauty In — *page 81*
Lovely Woman in the Lake, My Wife, My Love — *page 82*
When We the Velocities of Wonder — *page 83*
The Sad Mathematics of Our Lives — *page 84*
Driving the Drumlin Road By Jocelyn's At Dusk — *page 85*
Fat Little Girl Singing in the Lake — *page 86*
Watching Dusk Fall in the Cottage Yard — *page 87*
Listening to Peacock Point on a Summer Night — *page 88*
By the Shore's Collapsing Waters I am Bound — *page 89*
Waking On a Summer Morning — *page 90*
Last Night it Thundered — *page 91*
Queen Anne's Lace — *page 92*
5 Times Out of 9 — *page 93*
Neither a Leader Nor a Follower Be — *page 94*
While the Night Pulls Up Its Roots — *page 95*
The Last Crucifixation of a Fly — *page 96*
Forgive the House that Makes Him Wake — *page 97*
Saint Dog — *page 98*
Beyond Our Dogs — *page 99*

The Echo of Your Words Has Reached Me
I Too Can Show the Way — *page 102*
first impression from the air — *page 103*
Inuit Graveyard, Iqaluit — *page 104*
"I gave her a fox fur, and am ashamed" — *page 105*
The Place Where Poets Pause — *page 106*

Thor and Odin — *page 107*
Dancing on Wind — *page 108*
Wise Rage — *page 111*
Mountain Avens — *page 112*
Ten-Thousand-year-old Winter — *page 113*
Older Men Speak of Food — *page 114*
Midnight on Summit Lake with Mount Bredalblik — *page 115*
Never Again — *page 116*
Starless and Blue at Midnight — *page 118*
The Stone Bothy — *page 119*
The Ravens of Baffin — *page 120*
All Summer in the Light — *page 121*
A One-Beard Journey — *page 122*
Where are You now Cathy Jeanne — *page 123*
Returning to Night — *page 124*

An Almost Silent Drumming
Rumours of Police — *page 126*
The Orchard at the End of the Wind — *page 128*
Soweto and Souwesto — *page 131*
False Lions — *page 133*
Sitting Poolside in Suburban South Africa — *page 135*
Sudden Fascination — *page 137*
Loneliness as an Art — *page 138*
In the Belly of the Ndebele Village — *page 139*
Taken — *page 141*
Automatic Dogs — *page 143*
I Saw Them Walking in the Morning, ... — *page 145*
Rumpy Pumpy — *page 147*
Dark City — *page 149*
Refusing the Dark — *page 151*
My African Stone — *page 152*
An All, Most Silent — *page 153*
An Afterness — *page 155*

The Mission of Angels — *page 157*

In a Language with No Word for Horses
In a Language with No Word for Horses — *page 162*
A Dwindling Down of Dwellers — *page 163*
The Children of Brouage — *page 164*
The Lengthened Shadow of One Man — *page 165*
The Angels of the Self — *page 166*
The Six Month Winter of Isle Ste. Croix — *page 167*
The Dragons of Beyond the Known — *page 168*
Knives Over Water — *page 170*
A Shameless Girl, A Handsome Stranger — *page 171*
June 10th, 1613 — *page 172*
Time and Ptarmigan — *page 174*
Hélèn in Canada — *page 175*
The Poet Lescarbot — *page 176*
By What Was He Betrayed — *page 177*
The Startled Blue Flowers of Light — *page 180*
The Bones on Rue Buade — *page 181*

Though Their Joined Hearts Drummed Like Larks
From the Mouth of the Humber — *page 185*
The Intimacy of Canoe — *page 186*
From within the Yellow Engine of an Egg — *page 187*
A Priest Sees Étienne Brûlé and a Native Woman in the Night — *page 192*
Étienne Brûlé's Reply to the Priest — *page 195*
Father Joseph De La Roch Daillon's Journey Among the Neutrals, 1627 — *page 196*
Sad Song — *page 201*
The Cannibal Coffin — *page 202*
After His Death — *page 203*
Walking on an Ocean Beach at Dawn — *page 204*

Bright Red Apples of the Dead
This Morning, My Father — *page 206*
Newspaper Photograph of My Father … — *page 208*
When You're Down on Your Knees in a Field Called Forever — *page 210*
Somewhere Inside My Father — *page 212*
Most Nights Weeping — *page 214*
The Man with One Hundred Watches — *page 216*
The Art of Shaking Hands — *page 217*
Bright Red Apples of the Dead — *page 219*
Trucker Angels — *page 222*
Child's Time — *page 224*

Thirty-Three-Thousand Shades of Green
The Day the Planes Flew In — *page 228*
Until the Stars That Are Not There Have Disappeared — *page 230*
The Photograph Is Actually That of David Peel — *page 232*
America the Beautiful — *page 234*
A Dark Little Psalm Against War — *page 236*
Taking the Pulse of the Tortured Man — *page 237*
Thirty-Three-Thousand Shades of Green — *page 238*
Watching the Italians — *page 240*
His Change of Heart When it Comes to War — *page 243*
The Covenant — *page 245*

But Where Were the Horses of Evening
But Where Were the Horses of Evening — *page 249*
Why Am I the One Taken for a Monk... — *page 251*
Walking with Brother Paul — *page 253*
Alone — *page 256*
Washing the Cheese — *page 259*
Monks of the Mammoth Caves — *page 260*
Where Silence is the Light — *page 261*

Simply to Be Seen — *page 263*
Loosening Green–An Excursion at the Monastery — *page 265*
Something So Ugly — *page 267*
God Bless — *page 269*
The Colder Light — *page 270*
Walking Past Cow-Barn Lake — *page 271*
I Might Say — *page 272*
Living in the Monk Motel — *page 273*
What Burns Through Remember — *page 275*

Let Light Try All the Doors
Echo's Revenge — *page 278*
Handsome in Hanboks — *page 286*
What I Think — *page 288*
Sleeping Dictionary — *page 291*
Sex with a Second Woman — *page 293*
Bad Men Come — *page 295*
Tuk-tuks in Bangkok — *page 297*
Thai Boxer — *page 299*
Ten Days Out of Step with the Sun — *page 300*
Ghosts in the Mud — *page 302*
and thus beginneth the lesson — *page 304*
Being Human — *page 306*

One Leaf in the Breath of the World
Many the Wonders — *page 310*
The Horses of Bethany Hills — *page 311*
Undressing the Angels — *page 312*
Mustn't Complain — *page 314*
Operation Yellow Bird — *page 315*
Elegy for Al Purdy — *page 316*
One Leaf in the Breath of the World — *page 318*
The Silence of Secret Singing — *page 319*

The Semi-Permeable Rain-Soaked Tent of Sleeping — *page 320*
Blackout Thursday — *page 321*
Swearing in Church — *page 322*
Walking Bethany Hills Approaching Devil's Elbow — *page 323*
Black Sand Costa Rica early evening — *page 324*
The Fifth of Four — *page 325*
Mulberry Song — *page 327*
The Vanity of Grackles — *page 329*
Smashing the Sparrow — *page 331*
What Suffers into Shadow at the Edges — *page 334*
My Lost Sister — *page 332*
The Fourth Sparrow — *page 333*
The Lost Hawk — *page 335*
The Beauty of the Birdless Cage — *page 336*
Talk of Trees — *page 337*

Adoration of the Unnecessary
Seiche—Long Point Bay, Port Dover — *page 340*
Wild Blue Caterwaul — *page 341*
Briefly Beautiful — *page 342*
Solving Sarah's Riddle — *page 343*
Watching Two Cormorants in the lake in late January — *page 344*
Master Dogstorm — *page 345*
Feliz Navidad — *page 347*
Contemplation of a Dead Loon on the Beach at Long Point Bay — *page 348*
In my lonesome craft — *page 349*
Desire on the Wind — *page 351*
Modeling Borrowed Swimsuits at Christine Shinohara's House — *page 352*
Adoration of the Unnecessary — *page 353*
Evidence of life lying in the sand... — *page 354*
Nymphae — *page 356*
Toad — *page 357*
Beyond the Seventh Morning — *page 358*

Oh Be My Most Strange Valentine — *page 359*
Familiar — *page 360*
White Lake Moon — *page 361*
Here Where the Stone Remembers the Shell — *page 362*
Paper Wasp Nest — *page 363*
And I Stare at Everything in the Absence of Light — *page 364*

This Is How We See the World
This is How We Sometimes Share the World — *page 366*
A Life So Different from Mine — *page 367*
Lalo's Walls — *page 369*
The Last Supper — *page 371*
In the Colonial Regions of Lima — *page 373*
In the Catacombs of St. Francis, Lima, Peru — *page 374*
All Too Often — *page 376*
Lords of the Gutter — *page 377*
Golden Light of the Sun, Silver Tears of the Moon — *page 378*
Ya–Now — *page 379*

Counting Cranes
Mu—Not—lament for the lost kingdom of I am — *page 382*
A dream I dream on my first night in Beijing — *page 385*
Is Beijing burning — *page 386*
A boy speaks of his childhood in the countryside outside of Beijing — *page 388*
Undeserving blue — *page 390*
Tea flower falling — *page 392*
Climbing the Great Wall of China — *page 394*
Counting cranes — *page 396*
The empty boat — *page 398*
The Chinese on the moon — *page 399*
I thought I was in China held against my will — *page 400*
Suseok—viewing stones — *page 401*
An incident of the bridge on no return — *page 403*

The outset — *page 404*
Timmy's down the well — *page 406*
Broken time traveler — *page 409*
The insatiable hungers of the sun — *page 411*
last night we were speaking of spiders — *page 413*
Going back to the world — *page 415*

Traveling Through Each Other's Lives
Forgetful — *page 420*
The Ungoable — *page 421*
On the Beauty of Being Elsewhere — *page 424*
One Morning in Mayabe — *page 425*
El Hombre Con La Guitarra Azul — *page 427*
Broken Money, "Bazuk Para" — *page 429*
Writing the Darkness — *page 432*
The Truth of the Field — *page 435*
Lifeless–the Rose of the Heart — *page 438*
The Hummingbird Moth — *page 441*
Massingy-Les-Vitteaux, Burgundy, France... — *page 443*

They Murdered Our Sons While We Dreamed
They Murdered Our Sons While We Dreamed i – vii — *page 448*

Afterward:
To a Fiend (owning my juvenilia) and beyond...
Even at the Worst of Times — *page 458*
Thoughts of a Mouse at High Tide — *page 462*
My Alibi for an Eventful Wednesday in May — *page 463*

Bio Notes about the Author – *page 472*

Forward by Roger Bell

It has been almost forty-three years since I first met John Lee at Althouse College, Western University. It was there where we began our friendship, there where he, an already established and assured poet, began to mentor me in my writing, which at that time was barely tentative, timid, unassured. I owe him much for these decades of sage advice that have helped me find my voice, so of course when he asked me to write a forward to this book, I assented. I thought, "Sure, it will be easy. What don't I know about John and his writing?" After all, I'd read almost all these poems, listened to many of them over kitchen tables and early morning coffee, over beers on the shore at Peacock Point, Port Dover, Meldrum Bay, Port Elgin. On car trips to Kentucky or California, train trips to Ottawa, plane trips to Burgundy, ego trips where we attempted to outdo the other poetically.

But when I began to look at this massive compilation I began to question my original supposition. I started to see far more than the familiar; I encountered a writer of greater scope, and poetry even more profound and wide-ranging, than I was accustomed to. When you have finished this book (and I urge you to do so slowly, re-reading and savouring its nuance as you go) you too will see John Lee's wide and deep observations of this wondrous life. This is how he sees the world, and as we are drawn in, how we too begin to see it.

You will find that he isn't afraid to be playful, cheerful, light in his touch, as he begins with Poems For One or More Feet. He asks of you: *read this poem/ to set yourself free*. He requests that you *imagine each line/ hammering on the floor/ like a spoiled child.* He shows you irreverence. *Toes look up to you.* But then he demonstrates his power by jerking you back to sobriety with the final line of the section: *Your toenails die last.*

For it isn't Lee's cheekiness that predominates in this volume, although you will find elements of joie de vivre everywhere. But what you will really see is the gravitas he brings to his vision of this world. He is unafraid, as good writers all are, to point out that we are always on the verge. He keeps us aware of the fact that we are mortal. He doesn't want you to crumple under that awareness, but he wants you to recognize it, to accept it. He notes that *the heart plays its erratic melody.* Reading that, you place your own hand on your chest just to check. Disconcerted, you ask yourself: Am I still alive? He talks in almost painful terms of a jogger struck by a car who becomes a *pinwheel who comes down all angle of bone.* He describes with pity but unblinking accuracy *an old man empty/ as a dead woman's thimble.* He laments a sister who died in infancy: *the season of your birth/ outlived you.* We learn of his aging uncle, a formerly strong man failing: *when you're down on your knees in a field called forever.* That image is one to humble the proudest. He tells of his father's last plaintive, and we assume, unrequited, wish: *I want one red apple.* Don't we all want something so sensory at the end? But will we get it? He says of the dead: *we carry their ghosts on our breath/ like smoke*, an image both hauntingly beautiful but also enough to make you despair because those you loved will evanesce. You will never hold them. And then you too will whisper away.

You might think from that last paragraph that perhaps all is sorrow and despair in the poetry of John Lee but nothing could be farther from the truth. He is a poet constantly in search of satisfaction, of good, of beauty, and, usually finding it. He says, quite replete, *I'm God's enoughness/ for a while.* He experiences this enoughness all around him, in both the familiar and the foreign. Lee grew up on a farm in Kent County, in Southwestern Ontario and that rural side of him appears often. *I owe the earth such gratitude/for this briefly borrowed dust.* He takes you away to Costa Rica and eloquently describes the richness of bird life there: *heaven fits the sky.* He tells of the wild dogs of Peru and the respect they engender, then comes back to the beauty of a dead loon at Long Point: *one wing fanned over/an otherwise open face of stone.* Always the farmer, though long gone from the farm, he is endlessly in tune with the natural world. He describes a storm pelting his home on Lake Erie, *the wind and rain arguing against glass.* He paints a scene in spring on Lake Erie with his wife sowing crown vetch: *but here/the world is sucking in its gut a little/waiting for open seed/to first pronounce the air.* He whisks you away again to verdant Western Kentucky where he walks *the shaken-silk summer of fields.* And in those far fields he praises in his music the bright rhythm of the creatures he encounters: *the cows/are the light on wild grass* and horses *that drum to the withers/in rivers of burning.*

Wherever John Lee takes us in this volume of poetry, be it China, Thailand, Korea, Baffin Island, Burgundy, or the shores of our Great Lakes, readers must be aware of the archetype of his journey. Yes, the physical voyage has weight, but it is really the interior journey, the progress of the soul, that counts. While he so fluently details the world around him, Lee is more deeply in search of the ch'i, the vital life force within, maybe God, maybe just meaning, but *something just beyond the circle of light.* When musing upon the impressive waters of the Great Lake above which he lives, he says: *there resides in me the true possibility of my soul/its memory alive at the very tuning fork/of Adam's resonant bone/receiving life and responding in kind/to that breath of grace.* He feels that *each small life/blinks its soul to signal God.* He seldom writes as if lost and alone; instead he exudes a universality, an acceptance a belonging, a benediction, imagines himself *barely belonging where I am/I am everywhere/pierced by a self-proving light.*

I thank John Lee for granting me the pleasure of revisiting this impressive work, for giving me the chance to see it, and him, afresh. Now you can start reading, can see him as I know him: *the writer/alone at an inner desk/his reverent attention/receiving first light like a better darkness/the one below the ink/impossibly perfect on the pure white page/in the held breath of unwritten moments/yet to come.*

Roger Bell is a poet
living in Tay Township

Je Suis Désolé, Lo Siento, I'm Sorry

"And now I can smirk at what some call poets "courage."
This is the only life I've ever owned."

From the poem "Bourgeois with Bag" by Sydney Lea

I was born and raised on a farm in the heart of *who-do-you-think-you-are* Southwestern Ontario. When I studied French, the first phrase I mastered was *je suis désolé*, when I took Spanish - *lo siento* - and like every truly *Canadian* child in my region I was trained in the art of apology, in my case by a loving mother who encouraged me to 'hide my light under a bushel' inquiring of me, "Why do you use the word 'I' so often?" as though my ego weren't always in need of a good dressing down. Mother mine, *je suis désolé, lo siento*, I'm sorry. I can't help myself. I was born to shine.

My favourite book as a child was a book of nursery rhymes, and my favourite poem therein was the verse "Baa Baa Black Sheep." I suppose this might be easily understood since sheep were first brought to our farm over one hundred years ago. My great-grandfather, my grandfather, my father and his brother were all shepherds of distinction. However, instead of dutifully following the bellwether of the flock of Lees who came before me, I left the farm to study English literature at university. Like a foundling of Leeland, I was born with a literary rather than a bucolic nature. I had the good fortune of knowing exactly what I wanted to do with my life after first reading Dylan Thomas's poem "Fern Hill." I discovered my own particular *avocation* having fallen deeply in love with reading poetry and with the craft of writing poetry. How then might I hide my light under a bushel? How might I avoid the unavoidable 'I' against which my mother had given wise caution, when that very same 'I', that small beacon of the examined self, that "who do you think you am – egoist" was calling my name.

Although *John B. Lee*, the 'I' of this sweet incarnation, became an enthusiastic practitioner of the writing of poetry, he has never chased the idea of being identified as a poet. When a hockey-playing friend of his asked, "Do you call yourself a poet?" Without hesitation he replied, "No. I'd far rather be referred to as someone who writes poetry than be called a poet." "I'm not surprised," the friend said seemingly pleased by that answer. After all, another hockey player once opined in something of a pique over a now long forgotten dispute, "You ain't nothin' but a fuckin' poet. You ain't never broke a sweat in your life."

When he was in grade one the younger of my two sons told everyone I was a truck driver. And although I did drive truck on the farm and then I drove truck during my summer employment as a park ranger in Rondeau, I am not now, nor have I ever been, a truck driver. Thinking I was a truck driver, his grade six teacher invited me to speak to the class on career day, but when he learned that rather than driving a big rig on the back roads of the county I was a writer, he canceled my speaking engagement, saying to my son, "I'm sorry Sean. I just don't think that the students would find your father's career as a poet to be of much interest." For her part, my wife sees me at my most quotidian. When a star struck young woman inquired of her, "What's it like being married to a poet?" Without missing a beat she said, "I don't care as long as he does the vacuuming."

*

When I began writing poetry I also envisioned seeing my poems in print. Although I kept my proclivity for writing poetry a secret for a very long while, at the very same time I dreamed of being a fly on the wall in a room observing someone reading one of my poems. I wrote poems longhand, transcribed them into typewritten script, and in so doing I imagined seeing them in print

- first in a magazine or a journal, then in a book with my name emblazoned on the cover, and perhaps, finally, I thought to see those poems included in an anthology studied by future generations. I've lived long enough to see all of these aspirations realized. Indeed, I have had good fortune as a writer. Although I could wallpaper a large room with rejection slips, my first published poem appeared when I was seventeen, and a literary publisher came knocking at my door requesting the manuscript that became my first book. Seventy-five published books later, I still answer the question "What is your favourite of all the poems you've ever written?" with "The one I'm about to write."

If the first impulse is to write, and the second impulse involves seeing that writing in print, perhaps the third might involve seeking out opportunities for sharing the poem on the page by becoming the poet on the stage. That is to say, "reading the poems you've written at a poetry reading." The writer of the poem becomes the performer of the poem and the imagined reader of the poem becomes a member of an audience – a rapt listener. Not everyone who writes poetry also learns to master the art of reading a poem aloud. Many poets, myself included, are introverts by nature with an enthusiasm for solitude. Writing after all is said and done is a solitary craft. When I write, I like to be alone at a desk, alone in the room, alone in the house, alone in the world, diving deep and letting the poem flow onto the page. And for the most part, when the writing goes well, I'm not there when it happens. I vanish into the work.

*

It has been said that the fear of public speaking is the greatest of all human fears. Some psychologists suggest that it is even greater than the fear of death. Little wonder then, that poets might suffer stage fright. There was one occasion when we were reading poetry around a campfire. I happily introduced the next reader, a former student of mine. Upon hearing his name, he leapt to his feet, dashed across the yard, ran into the street, and raced down the road out of sight chased by the family dog, never to return for the remainder of the evening. "Where'd he go?" Someone asked. "Away," came the answer.

As an aspiring writer, I learned to master the fear of public speaking, though I remain an anxious performer. I am always nervous before any kind of speaking engagement. When I confessed this fear to my mother, she inquired "Why do you do it then?" If I dare to look back now on my grade eleven self, recalling the weeks of lost sleep, the days and days of anxiety leading up to the moment I strode to the front of the classroom, the paper quivering in my hand as I was required to deliver a speech, or read a brief passage from Shakespeare, or recite a soliloquy from memory ... I would call the man I've become a liar. Over the years I've read my work all over the world. Some of those readings have been high points in my writing life, and some have been disasters.

On the occasion of my first poetry reading, having overcome stage fright, I learned to love the experience and to bask briefly in the afterglow that comes when the reading has gone well. As a very young undergraduate student, I once read in professor Don McKay's university poetry class. Professor McKay complimented me on how entertaining I had been. And then he cautioned me, "Beware of your audience. It can ruin the work." That is not the only thing I've learned by reading poetry. I've also learned to honour the audience. I've come to believe that the poet is there for the sake of the audience, not the other way round. To quote friend Marty Gervais, "Attending a dull poetry reading is very much like taking a bad drug." He whispered these words to me while we watched drool form and drip from the lip of a listener who had dropped into a deeply somnolent snore sitting as he was within spitting distance of the reader who was droning on and on oblivious to his own affect upon the drowsy crowd. A bad poetry reading is not always the fault of the reader, but more often than not it is. The reader reads too long. The reader has failed to prepare. The reader cannot be heard. The reader says, "Just one more poem," the voice lifting and then not waiting for an answer forging ahead. The reader emotes, wags a finger, lets an arm drift in the air, affects a kind of tonal importance on undeserving words, breaks into a flop sweat, drones and fusses, gives a long and seemingly pointless preamble, never looks up from the page, ignores the list of those who have not yet read, eats time in gluttonous gulps. The greatest compliment a reader can receive comes when someone in the audience is overheard saying, "I am so glad I came. I only wish they had all read longer."

I am reminded here of the occasion when a visiting American poet stood up at the back of the room, strode purposefully down the centre aisle past the audience, past the host, placing his dapper fedora firmly on his head as he raced away saying to himself in a voice loud enough to be heard by all, "I can't take it any more" as he bolted out the door walking visibly and purposefully down the street his flight clearly visible through the plate glass window of the bookstore as the host turned importuning his guest, "But Robert, you're the featured reader. And besides, I haven't read my new work yet." Then as though the featured reader's desperate departure were simply a blip in the proceedings the host turned his attention back to the page in front of him and continued to read for another fifteen minutes without a pause. Little wonder then, that a friend of mine calls such readers "the angels of death." I've seen an entire audience stand up and leave at the intermission. I've heard a child blurt out,

"I don't like this poetry stuff!" I've seen on the clouded over face of someone in attendance affecting this awful resolve – *never again*.

That said, I've had far too many wonderful experiences to let those low points steal my joy. Better a bad poem than a good bomb. Better a tedious poetry reading than a thrilling riot. Over the years I've had the privilege of participating in and being featured reader at events that have been high points in my life.

I've had the privilege of reading for UNEAC (National Union of Writers and Artists of Cuba) in the courtyard of their headquarters in Holguín, for the English Department of Witwatersrand University in Johannesburg, South Africa, for a student conference for inner city children from the environs of Chicago at the Stephen's Point satellite campus of the University of Wisconsin, at a Northern Voices conference hosted by the University of Maine, and each of these readings was something of a personal apotheosis. If I close my eyes I can hear myself saying, "Esta poema tienne los moscas como los moscas aqui," as I prepare to read my poem "Counting the Flies on Pablo Casals," translated into Spanish and read in Spanish by my Cuban friend Manuel Léon. How might I ever have anticipated this moment, given my adolescent fear of public speaking? How indeed! I am a most fortunate human being.

I've been Poet Laureate of the Briars where I spent the morning touring the golf coarse with celebrities, at noontime noshing with famous personalities, in the afternoon sitting in Peter Gzowski's cottage on Lake Simcoe writing a poem to be read at the evening gala dedicated to the promotion of literacy. A television producer in the audience at that event invited me to write four poems to be featured on a major year-end program celebrating Canadian heroes. The emcees for that particular presentation were soon to be senator Pamela Wallin and future member of parliament Peter Kent. At the rehearsals a small audience sat in bleachers behind the camera and I did my best reading of the four poems I'd written. The listeners applauded as the director emerged from his glass booth at the back of the room. "How do you think that went?" he inquired. I was proud of the flawless delivery having read the poems without pause or stumble. The audience beamed. I said, "I guess I'm happy with it." "As a matter of fact it was awful." He said. "This is television, not the theatre. Go for something less theatrical, more natural." He encouraged demonstrating what he meant by giving my words a flat delivery thereby leveling out the dictionary music of my language. I complied and he was pleased. "Is that the way you plan on dressing?" He asked. I looked rather poetic, I thought to myself having donned my best trousers and most dashing floral vest. "Yes," I replied being careful to give an interrogative lift to my inflection. "Don't you have anything less garish, something more conservative, something in *brown*?" I haven't worn brown since my father dressed me. "Wardrobe will buy you an outfit." They purchased a pair of tan corduroy trousers and an expensive fine wool-knit sweater. "Everyone is envious of your sweater," the wardrobe assistant said handing me the item of clothing I would wear once and once only. I read my poems from the teleprompter. They did a second take in case there was something wrong with the first take. I watched from the wings as Pamela Wallin stepped up on the box set beside the rather tall by comparison Peter Kent. The rest is history. The rest is politics.

The first time I appeared on Morningside with host Peter Gzowski, we were still living in Brantford. In light traffic the studio on Front Street is an hour drive door to door. I was due to go on air at ten a.m. I left the house that morning at six thirty thereby giving myself plenty of time to arrive, get parked, scout out the location, and perhaps have a coffee and a bagel before the show. Unfortunately the traffic was heavy, a blizzard struck, construction narrowed the lanes of traffic, and the cars were backed up all the way from Burlington to Toronto. The QEW was a parking lot. We crawled. I prayed "Dear God. Don't do this to me. You wouldn't give me the opportunity of a lifetime and then steal it by sending a blinding snowstorm. Please let me arrive on time." As it happens, I pulled to the curb at Union Station, gave the wheel to my harried wife, leapt from the vehicle, piled into a taxi cab importuning him to take me to the CBC studio. I didn't know it was less than a block from where he was parked. He refused to drive me there. I insisted, offering a healthy tip. He drove me the fifty meters to the studio door, accepted my ten spot without a smile telling me to get the hell out. I raced through the lobby, took the elevator to the floor for Morningside. Ran breathlessly into the studio and I was rushed into a room where I sat down behind a microphone. I wiped the sweat from my brow, Gzowski entered and I said to him as he sat down, "My aunt Stella says hello." Gzowski had worked in Chatham as a young reporter and my aunt had been personal secretary to a local architect who was a close friend to Gzowski. The red light went on, "Tell me about your aunt Stella," he said. My wife told me that his producer threw the script in the air so the pages fluttered up and fell back to the floor. "There he goes again," she said. "I don't know why we even bother to prepare for these interviews." We did get around to talking about the book I'd come to promote, but only after we'd cleared the deck concerning aunt Stella, and Peter Gzowski had tried to stump me by challenging me to identify the four faces painted on the side of a building in downtown Brantford. When he asked me why he hadn't been included in an anthology I edited on hockey writing, I said, "Because you didn't make the cut, Peter." He was a good sport. I would be back two more times to appear on the radio program with the largest audience in Canada.

I had the privilege of reading on several occasions at the Milton Acorn Memorial Peoples' Poetry Festival in Prince Edward Island, having won the Acorn Award three times. My sons were both impressed when Cedric Smith who played Uncle Alex on Road to Avonlea crossed the room to say hello. He wanted to pick my brain on some rural concern in a script for the show. I shared the stage with him in Charlottetown and then performed together on guitar singing my songs written for children. Playing guitar with Cedric Smith was something I could not have anticipated all those years ago when prior to attending a Stratford Festival performance of Hamlet I had accompanied a few of my friends and gone to the Black Swan coffee house where Smith was featured along with Richard Keelan of the group The Perth County Conspiracy. My sister had one of their records with recordings of poems by Milton Acorn and Dylan Thomas set to music.

I also sang those songs on CBC Radio Windsor. When I was finished, the producer came out and said, "I guess if Leonard Cohen can sing, so can you." It may not have been intended as such, but I took it as a compliment.

I also took it as a compliment when two ladies said of me at a reading I gave to a poetry group in Dundas, "Doesn't he look just like Paul McCartney." "Oh doesn't he just." My wife still giggles to think of that occasion. The host for that reading was an elderly gentleman wearing an ill-fitting wig. His hearing was quite bad and for an aid, he chose to employ an old fashioned hearing trumpet that looked like the Victrola from ads for His Master's Voice. "Eh? Eh?" He inquired. "What'd she say?" "She said, 'doesn't he look just like Paul McCartney.'" "Who?" "Paul McCartney. Doesn't he just?" So much for poetry! My wife still loves to tell that story whenever she wants to take the puff out of my ego. I, on the other hand, don't mind to think that some might consider the resemblance I bore in my youth to the cute Beatle. Not that I ever looked like Paul McCartney. But to those two ladies with the English accents, I looked enough like Paul to inspire the compliment. Never mind moon, June, spoon. As I write this, I'm wearing the face I keep in the jar by the door. Those are the highlights.

And yet I have had low moments.

There was the occasion when I was reading in a high school classroom and the door burst open as a hired clown came tap dancing into the room delivering a birthday gram to a girl in the audience. There was the occasion when I was running through the chill rain of a Halifax night putting up posters on the way, arriving late and drenched to the skin to be greeted by an empty room. The door opened, a gaggle of people entered taking their seats. One of them said, "Isn't this the square dance class?" "No," said the library host. "That is upstairs." Imagine my delight when the caller began his calling and the ceiling began to shake and writhe with the cowboy boot rhythms of a hoedown. "Okay, you can start reading now." There was the occasion when I was invited to read at a bar in Seoul, Korea. What I didn't know, and what the owner had not given thought to, was the fact that this was the same night as the world cup soccer semi finals between Korea and Turkey. The poetry crowd sat at a table away from the bar and the soccer fans sat at the bar watching the match on TV. Unbeknownst to me the bartender turned the volume off on the television so I might be heard reading my poems. A near riot ensued and my life was being threatened without my knowledge. I ended up reading at a table in the street with the costermongers selling their wares and stopping in wonder at what I was doing. There was the occasion when I was a featured reader at a bar in Windsor. There was a long list of readers that night, every one of the opening readers had been told to read for a maximum of two minutes. One of the readers read for forty minutes, and then apologized to me saying, "Sorry I can't stay for your reading, John. I have to go." At the moment I took the stage, the door burst open and into the bar came an entire baseball team celebrating their victory in an end-of-season tournament. The click clack click clack of their ball cleats crossing the floor sounded like the threshing of grain. "Excuse me," said the host. "We're doing a poetry reading here." I begged them for two minutes indulgence. They quieted down and when I was finished they applauded and went back to their revelry. Needless to say, I did not read for the twenty minutes allotted me as feature reader. There was the time the library was closed and we were locked out. The audience was arriving, and I was the host. The librarian had left town and the person he left in charge of opening the venue had *gone to the movies* I was told when I managed to contact someone. We decided to host the reading at my home. I brought my guitar amp down to the living room, hooked up a microphone, had a friend shuttle the audience from the library to my house, and we held the reading in my suburban residence with people sitting in every chair, standing shoulder to shoulder in the kitchen, sitting on every step of the stairway going up to the second floor and down to the basement, and we made do

 My wife tells me now that that particular occasion was her favourite of all the readings she's ever experienced. To me, it felt like a disaster. I cursed the librarian from the bully pulpit of my parlour calling him all kinds of awful. And when he arrived at my doorway having driven all the way to Brantford from Toronto, I insisted that I would accept his apology on one condition. That he remain for the duration of the reading, and that he give an accounting of himself, thereby exculpating me of any guilt. He stayed. We read. The audience hung around for quite some time after the reading drinking my beer and partaking in the bounty we provided.

I have to confess that my wife was correct. That particular reading which seemed to promise to be a disaster turned into a gala event. And for every sour note, for every poor showing, for every low moment, there have been dozens of delights. Though there was the time at the annual poetry festival in Austin Texas where I was the featured Canadian poet when a pretender crashed the reading brandishing a knife threatening the host with this lunatic ultimatum, "Either I get to read my poems tonight or someone is going to die!" Fortunately he was disarmed and evicted from the premises. As a Canadian I wanted to say to him, "Je suis désolé. Lo siento. I'm sorry." But that is a flop sweat for another occasion.

Poem for One or More Feet
(1974)

for John Tyndall without whom this poem would have been a shoebox, or a small explosion of foot-sounds on a fire escape

for Margaret Avison whose feet, though I've never seen them, have left their impression in my brain like coins in wax

for Cathy always, whose feet have been a constant inspiration

... how to read this poem:

This poem
is a dance
a ritual
imagine each line
hammering on the floor
like a spoiled child
or spinning an insane dervish.
Imagine yourself as one
or all of these lines.
Imagine the poem closing you in
like a cell

read this poem
to set yourself free

Prologue:

I retrieved this poem
from the rubble of my notes
as a child
would pluck a dead cat
from a demolition site.

I hold it swinging in air
like the scales of Athena
over my last conquest.

This poem
like the only moving part
in a Swiss timepiece
divines itself.

Poem for One or More Feet

Welcome to these footprints
stripped of sock, shoe
and boot –
just five toes apiece
decked out in nails
and twitching like nervous
    fingers
from death's last throes.
Sing them with tapping
or dancing
heels.
Thump them out
like a snowshoe rabbit
careful not to skip a beat.
Stand on them
sweating
as the osmosis
informs *your* feet
with a black trail of lines.
Wear holes in them
with the repeated rhythms
of your soul.
Wear them like shoes
or a second skin.
Walk them in the street
not like dogs
but like birds –
watching them as they flit
from hat to hat
landing with a flash of light
only for an instant.

Study them
like an orthopedist.
Wake each day
looking at your feet
and remind them
that this is their poem.

Why a Foot Should Be a Poem

According to
a conservative estimate
there are twice as many feet
as people for people
with the notable exception
of handicaps
and four times as many
feet
as dogs for dogs
and one hundred times as many
feet
as centipedes for centipedes
so why not write
a poem about feet
for feet

Inspiration

my feet
grounded in truth
like grapes into wine
swell and bruise
with inspiration

imagine yourself
without feet
just a poem
at the end of each leg
waiting for this poem
to swallow it

Voices That Feet Have

Feet sing
street songs
poems flowing
sole to sole
like a jangle of mispronounced words
come stalking
in a death march
or a parade

The Uncloven Foot

Feet usually travel in pairs
cleaving
like breasts
or Chicago cops

but sometimes feet
travel in clumps
like sludge mud
in a creek belly
these feet belong
to centipedes
or (a) crowds of   people
   (b) packs of   dogs
   (c) herds of   cattle
   (d) flocks of   sheep
   (e) murders of crows
   (g) gaggles of   geese

and, even if alone in appearance
they're still
accompanied by a limp

Phasing

Consider how
the quintessence of soil
 (mud or dirt)
seeps in through the soles
of your feet
or infects
your entire body
like the mad spurt
of oil
that sends your car
sprawling in the air
for inspection
your head
(like the car)
coming to a stop
in just the right place

Point C

I move
from Point A
to Point B
and my feet
like a fine pencil
join the dots
in habit response
or as a hand
maneuvering
a pawn
in a crucial game of chess
informing one of design
proportion
and
Point C

A Foot for All Seasons

Brown feet
and rain in grey sky
the magic mud
webbing toes
like a confused spider
making her home
in the beak of a hawk

White feet
and blue sky
summer day and green grass

White feet
and chafing
redyellowbrowngreen
                        flesh
like a beautiful bird
mating
in the dirt and mud

Blue feet
and the cold wind
singing like a bird
in the trees
ice forming nails
on your scaly flesh

The Path Taken

Feet that long
to kiss the soil
or to paddle
like ducklings
in water and oil.

Feet that laze
like cows in the sun
or like
foolish children
in the rain run.

Feet that toil
in shoes
like an old black beggar
soaked in booze
and rhythm and blues.

Feet
that wear dirt
like a mothy
old coat
or a grey tattered shirt.

Feet that remember
everything
like a withered old man
with a pipe and a story
in a porch swing.

Feet that call you
master
following you
like faithful dogs
to one final forgivable
disaster.

Feet that live and die with you
And still you say you die alone.

Feet-ish Journals

Hypothesis:

The feet are the most sexually sensitive organs of the body. Nurture them Properly and you will trigger a rapid fire of multiple orgasms each one comparable to the most notorious ever imagined in the most smut-luscious journals of antiquity.

Observation:

The feet are at one extreme of the body – the brain is at the other.

Conclusion:

Since the nerve impulse must travel the entire length of the body and back again merely for something as miniscule as an itch or a wound, the erogenous potential of the feet is mindboggling.

Remarks

My feet adore
your feel
tiny
and homely
as crumpled paper
naked toes
sizing
one another up
we walk together
in each other's
footprints
like docile sheep
grazing
in a pasture.

Loving Feet

Four feet lay in a room
two facing two
left laced in right
and right in left
little strange feet
moving in the night
like cats
the sheets
settling in finally
clouds
after one last
clap
of thunder.

Fetus

The feel of feet planted in the soil like two fine strong seedlings, punching the dust, or mud, or snow with five toed roots that squirm with unnatural life, like half-eaten things, these feet sent spinning like tumbleweed by a single fist that strikes and blurs them in the sun. I stand upright watching as the pride that was your feet is torn like a ball and chain from your ankles and turned unnaturally to the freedom that comes with humiliation.

Requiem for Feet Lost in Battle

Armies of feet
blasting our battlements
with foot powder
their spray balms
fogging the air
with a sickening
sweet smell
of perfume. One brave
foot soldier
sallies
to the fore
cocks his big toe
like a gun
in respect
only to catch a fragment
of shoe leather
in the quick
just beneath the nail
and has to be carried off
limping.

The Knife

The knife
nibbles
the flesh
that webs his toes
like a hungry bug
gormandizing a leaf.

"Cancer,"
the surgeon said
as he held it up –
the webbing –   swinging
looking like an earlobe
or and eyelid
not even slightly resembling
a foot
or a deviant poem.

Inscription Found on an Instep

your soul is a slave to truth
free it

Portrait of the Artist as a Young Foot

Two dolphin like objects
fish with four fins each
or dorsalled
and ventricled
	unwebbed
and one huge
gill –
a balance keeper.
Psychotic toe
decked out like a Chinese emperor
veins tracking humped backs
like rivers – dendritic and silent
sans fish and sunlight
and open air.
Subterranean arches
dangle stalactite fibers
like children
dangling fish skeletons
in front of cats.
Ankles
stuck out like hubcaps
or mutant breasts
	sans nipples
	sans milk
	sans chests.
And flesh drawn up
like a sock
or a winter cap
or the hide of a hounds face
black as cattails
and blind as shoe leather.
Deaf as the pile carpeting

tasteless as Adam's ale
wrinkled and ugly
as half-eaten prunes
haggard as corn husks
and tired as mud

Facts You Should Know

i

To your feet
the sky begins on the ground
luminous insects embossed
like stars in the dirt

ii

Footprints track your soul
like a path of celestial stars

iii

to your feet the ground is a woman
(or a man)
moving beneath them
their toes humping the dust

iv

toes are like insects
toenail shells
like exoskeletons
defying the elements

v

toes like city punks
travel in packs

vi

toes look up to you

vii

your feet are almost always
born last

viii

you have four crotches on each foot

ix

your feet are able to go higher
than your head
though your head can seldom go lower
than your feet
in which case you'll
be rendered senseless anyway

x

without feet
a mile
might have been
52,160 noses
or 12, 865 fingers

xi

your toenails die last

To Kill a White Dog

The captain steers the glass tour boat around the shallows of the Grand River. In the heart of corn country, the home of Pauline Johnson is a proud reminder of how Canadians have always treated the Indians decently and with respect.

Speaking into the small microphone he begins another story, the heroic tale of one pioneer whose bravery and perseverance were so great that an Ontario town on the river now bears his name. Chagard. He came to settle in this country with the dream of farming his own land. This brought him into conflict with the Indians.

By an unfortunate coincidence Chagard settled on the very spot where the local band of Indians gathered in the spring for the annual celebration of the end of winter. The festivities involved the ritualistic killing of a lone white dog as a sacrifice to the gods.

Chagard was forced to defend himself against vicious Indian attacks. On two occasions his buildings were burned and he was seriously injured. But Chagard stayed put. He lived a long and fruitful life. He is one of many pioneers whom we in Brant County are proud to call ancestor.

*

An interested listener asks a single question:

What is your source?

All of my sources are primary.

*

To Kill a White Dog

"Shall I at least set my lands in order?"

Barely here and already toiling them under.
Plough leaving ass-crack furrow.
Already you are marking off the field's perimeter.
Looking at the trees, they grumble
And shuffle back, a mean crowd behind a rope.
Looking at the river you have met
A long brown snake you can't stare down.
Chagard, you come dreaming rectangular.
The geometry of your hauteur will not include
The proud pine. Your axe will cut him through
And blast the stump. You have invented agriculture.

You told the Indians your rights
Are guaranteed by the King's English. You built a house.
A barn. You improvised. Like magic
Great bovine beasts with teats like fingers
Sprung from your fingertips. A wife was penciled
Into the margin of your ledger. From her
You made clay replicas of children. They must learn
That God breathes life into the yellow dust.
Hand that begs for manna.
You told the Indians of these marvels.
The missionary position is the only position.

You must have told them 69 times
The evil of screwing bears.
You built your barn exactly
Where they killed the white dog.
You told them it was foolish to try to kill winter.
They just smiled with their snow-coloured teeth.
Simpletons, mystics, fanciful naked primitives.
They told you if you built your barn THERE
They would kill you, your family, your cattle.
They would murder you in your sleep.
Your blood would drain like melted snow.
Your face would burn like bear meat
Dropped in a fire. They told you to move
Your barn even after you built it. You did not reply.
You are not a gypsy. You have a concept of permanence.
You have abstracted heroism.
You have had a premonition of your own survival.

The first arrows tip-tapping like rain
Or a handful of pea pebbles tossed on a lake
Could not pierce your armour.
The cedar rib cage you fashioned out of fallen trees.
It was smoke, not fire that drove you
From the house. Fire you could consume,
Tear it from the wall like a ripe hide.
But the reeking, puffing gluttony of smoke.
The dark within the darkness of the fuming night.
The double blindness. The Shadow's mirror.
Drove you outdoors coughing, spitting up the murky gloom.
The first arrows came tip tapping
Like bee stings. A handful of hot glowing ashes.
They could not pierce the armour
You had concocted out of your personal wilderness.
You stagger, quivers rattling tree music.
A great whoop of stick-clicking death.
You shake and topple a muddle of bone jewellery.
Sure you are dead, the Indians strip and burn
Your barn till its ashes are snow coloured.

dream sequence — black and white — down and across

    the white dog   in the dark ash
    has managed   their destruction
    his own death   my foot stirs
    spitting up bones   and I see my face
    whole   as in a pool
    animals smashed
    in a froth   my daughter
    of blood   wears a dress
                                    of fire
    a green fly   the flames are black
    crawls in one nostril   they cast no light
    and out another   her heart
    the dog   is crawling
    has a fixed smile   from between her legs
    the sunlight   it has the eyes
    sticks to him   of a snake
    there is mud
    on his tongue   my wife
                                    fell to dust
    my mother   in my head
    is ice   like powdered snow
    she is stiff
    as a stick   in the dark
    frozen into the river   confusion
    she suckles the snow   of my survival
    at her breast   in the black
    it eats   ruination
    greedily   of my soul

    There is no celebration   There is no celebration
    only ice   only fire
    the gods   God
    are cruel   is good
    if you love   if you love
    the world too much   Him

Your wounds seal themselves. Seal your flesh.
You are preserved. Your flesh there
Is like the stitching on a mended doll.
In you fingers you hold a kernel of corn.
Yellow hard and angular, the hipbone
Of a miniature woman. In the corn you hold
Silk soft green unfolding leaves.
Spiky rustling ripe summer opulence.
You run your calloused hand along the side
Of the new barn, the curve of hewn longs
Like the inside of a woman's thigh.
Your house is erecting itself in the clearing.
Blistered and grassless where you have dragged
The great dismembered trees.
Transformed. Your dwelling. Your owning. Your mark.
The river is struggling to learn a foreign language.
Stuttering in its shallows over unfamiliar stones.
Trying to speak its new grand name.

A ghostly magistrate
In oak leaves walks the town site.
Here he plants the 5 and 10
That will suckle its flashing silver windows in the sun.
Here is the bank, the liquor store,
The ball park, the arena, the
Funeral parlour.
Here is the sign that bears your name.
Chagard, this town, the bastard child
Of your seed pumped into the ground,
A bullet into a rifle.

You who murdered ceremony, waited in your house
Like an apostle for the second coming, ignored the second coming,
Built your barn again, come from your grave and look
On this inheritance. Face your maker.
Face history. It wears a mask.
Face myth. It holds a mirror.

This is not what you anticipated.
But you did not come uninhabited to this bleak land.
A darkness rises in you. A clear blackness.
Moon on the deep. A warm Bible.
Smoke within smoke. Dream within dream
Within dream. You have kept the past
Pressed beneath rock.
It emerges. It pisses from you.
An astringent aura. The wilderness is.
Petrified. You have unfathered. The real.
Earth drops from your plough like flesh.
Plants crisp and die out of season.
Trees lean down but do not fall.
Stiff old men listening to a new age.
Weeds rush in green waves
Pricketted orgulous with the heat.
An ebb and flow.
Contending with the sun you kept
Like a wafer of butter in a golden pyx.
The sea dancing in a cruet.
The smallness of stars on a raven altar cloth.
The elements chiming in a music box.
God pinned on a trinket
From the cloisters of Europe
Fell into this black green abyss.
Where He might laugh like rapids
Or wail all night thrushing his grand throat
In a tree.

Chagard, still you traced
Your vermicular path to the river's edge.
Bent and startled the faceted brown water.
Yet this is not what your expected.
Your knees imprinting on the damp ground
Like skulls. A pagan genuflection.
Before the raucous indifference of the forest.
You saw yourself striding a treetop trail
To this place. Galvanic.
Lifting marble arms to the heavens.
The wilderness a ruffled dandy waltzing before you.
Not this ragged sun cockfighting in a clear sky.
Not this shagginess. Not this willfulness.
You press your faces to the water's brown skin.
Drink in silence. You are complete. Alone.

The soft-voiced arrows come a second time
Whispering on their slender breath.
The darling quills dipped in the red ink of your blood.
Underlined and wrote in the margins of history:
"This man
Has a heart that feeds on stone."
The good voice in the stone is silence.
It found and shattered the bone of all resistance.
It left a quaking petulance in your ribs.
It scribbled on your body. It gutted truth
Like a great beast. It skinned the resilient snake.
It left you purring in a froth
Where flies walk on the soapy
Red bubble machine of your last breathing.
Or so they thought, nudging the blatant drowsiness of death.
Cudgeling your cattle with clubs so their legs jerked
Like fatal masturbations. Scouring with fire
Your barn and house. Leaving you for the dogs
And the black crows with beaks like yellow claws.

The silence around you. Your heart chewing off
Its arteries, sawing your rib cage, tunneling out.
Whirling in a tangle of veins like a horse spooked in his reins.
Pumping the plump clots smooth. You should have died.

How could they leave you twice for dead?
They might have tortured, maimed, scalped, nutted,
Burned, buggered you on a sharpened stick.
The bitch of history was in heat. The crows were drooling
For carrion, honing their beaks in the tree crotch.
The river was eating its banks. It was enough.
It seemed enough. But you have a talent
For survival. Death is a whoring chrysalis.
The future was crystallizing your fate.
The snow dogs were whelping in the longhouse.
The sunrise was a fast flash
On the morning of your first consciousness.
When you looked at the river you saw a rainbow glass tour boat
Splashy with tourists flashbulbs popping like silver trout
On the surface. A loud speaker blared out
The home of Pauline Johnson and told how
People applauded on her first European tour.
This was not your first hallucination.
You saw her lift her dress and desecrate romance.
You saw her feet cloven and her thighs
Brown with soft hair. Even though she was unborn.
Undead. You saw her bricked in. She too will give her name
To things when she is ripe. Reduced to bone.
You saw her wrap the antlers in her skirts.
In this vision you forged the need
To be remembered. To remain. To stay put.

Bushed by the timbre of your voice
You lost track of the season's resonance.
God sent the sun squawking round each morning.
Bothered by His lack of indifference. His meddling.
Knitting rain shawls for the earth like a feisty grande dame.
Ruining the trees in the fall
Knocking down their crisp brown leaves
So their naked branches are black lightning upside down.
Letting a quarrel of snow squall in the clearing for days.
Encouraging the wilderness to creep back.
Damned by His incurable will to interfere
You wonder whose side He is on.
And at night when the insects come,
Like angels of hell, there is a stunted emptiness to enter.
And like a child you sit on your crude bed and drag the blunted
Stick of your imagination over the dirt floor of your cabin.
Square roots. Rectangular fields. Triangular rocks.
Conical pines. Even the sky and bush have a conscious edge.

The white dog has dropped his jaw in a new fire.
It will not burn. The white dog explodes
In the longhouse, his fangs driven like thorns
Into the black eyes of the children.
Indian women throw white dog after white dog into the inferno
Of an abandoned car. They go up in a whoop
Like fistfuls of gasoline. The white dog
Wearing asbestos boots walks on hot coals like a fakir.
The white dog has an ulcer and drinks too much beer.
The white dog swallows fire in a circus tent at the CNE.
The white dog was quaffing Dubonnet at the Coconut Grove
                                   when the fire started.
The white dog fiddled while Nero burned.
The white dog celebrates the end of celebrations.

A person who is reading with interest asks a single question:

What is your source?

My source is the river.
All my sources are primary.

*The Day Jane Fonda
Came to Guelph*

When This Old Poet Shambles Past

When this old poet shambles past
speaking his verse
like the fatherly drone
of a stormless sea

remember that once
long before he sorrowed the bloodless news of death
he lived by the pleasant melody
of each rubbed nerve
when the flesh slummed
like a buzzed cello string
in the hot moments
that muddled the head.

But they were all nameless, these nights
worn out with beauty
the ornaments of lived times
hung like garlic cloves and labellum
in a pantry rich with spice
before they fell asleep in books
grown stale with closet air
and lack of mind.

The Subtleties, Lunenburg, Nova Scotia

for Don Linehan

Two men there are:
the farmer and the fisherman.

Two ideas:
the land hard turned
and the sea's soft furrow.

Two ways:
drink and live and spend
wild times as wild and free
as water, wind, and sky
or rooted and close
as tree and heavy stone
to save and hold and own
with sober reckoning.

But when on this harbour I stand
to watch the boats come in
followed by gulls
lighting and taking flight
I remember the fresh-turned field
behind my father's spring tooth
alive with those same lake birds

and in this I see
the subtleties of God
and the glory of man.

Riding with Dick

I'm riding with Dick
in his old pickup truck
watching the road unspool
through the rusted-out floorboards
listening to the slappeta slappeta
of a tire bulge
as it follows the hard inescapable logic of asphalt

and I'm remembering
how once he strode
with a loaded pistol into a quiet cafeteria
strutted across the floor to an open door
and lifting the gun
let off three quick blasts
so the birds shot up from the pines
like cowardly milkmen startled by cuckolds.

"There's no brakes on this here truck
John," he shouts over engine noise
and to prove it
he tramps the pedal
grinning at me and grinding another ratio
so the cogs mesh hard
like a moron's tooth stumps.

I look across at Dick
life flashing before my eyes in that fast truck
while all around the sky
is blueberry stained and rushing
in a gust …
my heart is socking at my ribs
like a baseball tossed against brick
as I imagine myself cut in half
my torso watching my legs
running wild in the road
till they fall to beat out some final rhythm
like cat tails
when the sniff of mouse is fresh in the cheese.
Never again will I ride with Dick
who is grinning a grin
that cracks his face
and lifts his two wide-set ears
before driving away in that thrashing contraption
with a horse trough tub of live bait
sloshing in the back
the minnow popping at the sky
in tiny silver wishes
then falling back like jewels from broken bracelets.

This Poem for Nothing
– Ninety-two Second Bout

The boxer fell
into galaxies
on the mat
his slack frame
filled with bloodless gravity
emptied
in slow wobbles
found the corners
like a rat-snooped maze
beyond
the repetition of heartbeat
pumping an alphabet of p's
eyes holding
an ink stain of dark blue air
a single moment
like a blacked-in crossword square
then palm mumbles its heel
on canvas, curls
and monkeys with the buzzing ring rope
pulling at the primordial shapes
babied by light and shadow.

And for this sliver of humility
he is paid fifteen million dollars
while I give you this poem
for nothing.

Spring

Tom is sitting
on the halter box
shining brass buckles
lifting them one by one
from a dry water pail
by their moss-green leather straps
finished
he draws
each lead through oiled cheesecloth
leaving a shiny linseed smear.

The he drinks Dow ale
with his lips to the bottle
as if he'd blow a blue note
to run your spine length
like sweat.

Every spring
when rain whips the barn
like a lazy slave
there he'll be
bent over and slow moving with his black Brasso cloth
a half bottle of ale
beside him
that will last the afternoon
while puddles filthy as a smoker's spit
gather beyond the rickety door
and cats preen on feed sacks
like bored mistresses blowing their nails.

The Makers and the Spoilers

for John Lennon

There are the makers
and the spoilers.
The creators and the killers.
The unlucky vandals
with hearts like birdshit on the wind.
Like winter rain
in a grey canal.
Side streets unbuttoned
to traffic
and the scrimshaw of losers
carved in paint
with a car key.

The kiss-my-ass calypso strut
that tigers them
so you mustn't meet their fishbowl eyes
where the bruised silence swims
like unendurable
light
    knifing a mirror.

Their unconsulted embryos came to life
hissing each like a forged horseshoe
when the moon dropped
a quarter in a moviola night
with the rickety-rackety
of bed posts
against a chipped plaster wall
a train passing
on tilted wheels over hot rails
and heart fluttering like a bird in a cat's mouth

    in dark   assiduous
        corners
that fit
        their shoulders
like broken fragments refit
        and fidgeted.

Shadows shoot their missiles
play pat-a-cake on pavement
under the laid-out corpse
of a streetlamp shining
its booze-coloured skin.

What with all of us dying
why behave
like an attic bat in the torchlight?
Why cringe
and slap black hinged
careless of the radius of love?

Are you not pleased with the beautiful bollix
of life?   Must you prove God
wrong
at every turn?

Why should the good cry out
when the evil die?
Death is the kind of gift they might be denied.

Let them live forever
with old age smouldering in their sour flesh
like the stink of a wet fire
in a piss-soaked mattress.
Rudolph Hess blind, lonely, crippled with pain
dragged by the cramping hours
up a misery of days
towards the end ...

Lasciate ogni speranza voi ch'entrate
(and speaks the ghost)
Ihr wisst nichts von der zeit
(you know nothing of time)
nor the guilt of flowers
nor the light that shows me
where the hidden angels lie.

The Sequence

The world is a strange place
and there is nothing like the truth.

Nothing like dying on an anniversary
John Housman on the day celebrating his performance
in *War of the Worlds*
or dying on your birthday
Shakespeare, or the poor sot
who threw a spent beer keg on a fire
so it exploded
an aluminum shard severing his spinal chord
breaking the connection he had
with the living
in the firelight
the stars dropping on the grass around him
like sparks from a well-struck log.

Imagine
a dog
leaping from a balcony seven stories up
imagine
a hapless pedestrian
in a careless promenade
his head
strung to the dog's path in gravity
as if by an invisible comic guywire
imagine
a bus braking too late
        before a stalk-still figure
staring at the dog, the man
as if waiting
for the instant to snap into place

imagine a third man
running to the scene
his heart suddenly
and strangely caught
strangled in the tight net of a moment
in the act of stopping
the four dying together as though they had made a pact

or imagine a girl
reading, quietly
                    a grouse flying blind
STRIKING
the large picture window behind her
glass knifing
the room
shivering into the furniture
and into the carpet
like the last ice slivers
converging from a thousand spilled drinks
but for the small blood-tear on her cheek
she is safe
though the bird   dumb on the carpet
                like the severed head
                of a Gaul

anything can happen, and anything will

imagine
a room full of clerks
coolly, half-bored, discussing the efficient and systematic
extermination of Jews and gypsies –
NO! That is too horrible to be true
no one would ever believe ...

The Day Jane Fonda Came to Guelph

When Jane Fonda came to Guelph
factory smoke
twisted in the air like half-naked catalogue models
and the river
lay in its bed all day
pretending its name was Marilyn.
All rearview mirrors
played their best angles like yesterday's rushes
and birds fluttered in their nests
like nervous hatcheck girls
under a whiskey sun
that poured itself out in dark corners
where the wind was a breathy Hollywood blonde
looking to get laid for a cameo.
Every storefront lothario preened and posed
while outside of the city dogs sang in the far hills until dark.

Yes, when Jane Fonda came to Guelph
even under the loose and tumbling
shook-down hair of willowy late-autumn rain
everything sashayed
and grew important for a while.

Joggers

Joggers
run a gauntlet of desperate dogs
and
travel
mobile targets
for Sunday drivers shaking their hubs
like a verdict
in soft gravel.

Doug turning the pinwheel of his Reeboks
down from his fastened knees
blew from a van hood
like a butterfly
spun in a breeze

came down all angle of bone
striking the asphalt for the friction
of flesh
and the feel of the scar's pre-form
with his ballast tilting on the pistoling fingers
all the empty wallets of easy wounds
opening their moneyless flaps
till he made the final slow-motion splash
and settled on his lanky meat
like a storm-torn branch.

Few have known the thrill
of how an accident can plain an inch
of shim from a heel
or make the future obliterate
like ice water on hot glass
but joggers run
the weird currency of miles
while heart plays its erratic melody
like a striptease drummer
and dogs narrate the neighbourhood
or celebrate a sweat-sock thread
with fangs applauding
like an operatic curtain call of plastic bracelets.

Oh these joggers, they hear their deaths
as the calling of impatient mothers
and they are ever late for namelessness.

A Heavy Harmless Sorrow

He walks the thread
each day
tapping his cane
click-tap, click-tap, click-tap
the wingbeat of a branch
slow plucking clapboard
before a storm.

Careless in the trap of bones.
Cricket lean
his eyes pale as the struck-blue nails of the drowned
his hair hoarfrost
and clean, coon-clean his polished skin.

He rounds the neighbourhood
again and again
as if to weave a crooked web.
How sad he seems
and empty
as a dead woman's thimble.

He's lost and tumbled
like a beetle
on a leaning strand of grass
beneath the nail-pricked lid of a jar
this Sisyphus wound nudge the hours
up a flag of streets
all day
and never pause
but for when he rarely sits and talks to the heavens
or prints a crumpled zero
on the air
for looking through as if to cut from cloth
those brave realities
that persevere in other minds.

And now those other minds have come
to close a frame of ribs
upon each breath
and wreck each shape with words
sliding down the ruined tiles of wind.

He leaves to seek a lipless place
among the clamoring solitude
of walking   ever walking with his stick
like a cockroach in a hollowed egg.

Soundless Voices

Your life struck and flared and left
like a damp penny match.
Your body
barely scarred the earth.
The season of your birth
outlived you.
Your tiny bones lie broken in the clay
like dollhouse struts.
You are bent over a clock wheel
pulsing like a breathed-upon thread.
You are the tongued-up wind
that curls within the words
this poem holds.
You cannot fear what you have known
since first you peeped, your absence
unwound the trembling cog of your heart
a single notch
before it closed your pebbled fist
like a spider next a flame.

I, your brother
am bound by soundless voices
that drag this pencil
like a river
in the centre of the sea.

Spreading Crown Vetch

My wife is seeding crown vetch on the cliff
fighting where earth slid to the lake
wet days
slithering like a satin counterpane
with nothing to hold
but the watermark curve of clay seamed with ribs
like a half-starved horse
struck to the edge
where trees lean on the verge over roots
like tired old men
fastening galoshes' buckles on a low stoop

but here
the world is sucking in its gut a little
waiting for open seed
to first pronounce the air
with delicate inlaid tongues uncurled
against the heavy rage
and language of *mud*

When You are Gone Away

When you are gone away
it is like a key is missing from the world
though there be many doors
I would try
and many rooms unseen
without within
their handles gnarled like hickory and oak
and old man knuckles
burled arthritic in a crook
down to the withering yellow nail
hold, oh, they would open
like brandy bottles if you were here
in the too-close air
and bees would zoom down
about the blue eye of a little lake
a reflected wisp
that skims the surface
like a thought set free.

But you are gone away
and I am keyless as a fish
high in the knot of a tree
watching each golden door capsize
and darken
like a ring inside a glove.

I Wake to Breathe Your Beauty In

I wake to breathe your beauty in
your soft pink sex
mummed like a secret-keeper's mouth
the stone imprisoned by its fall
could no more hang upon the wind
that I hold back this love
your shape procures
a note so faintly played
upon the felts
it leaves no mark
like a dustless butler's glove
and I with sad melodies unsung
with wordless names and voiceless calling
dream the mild narcotic
of your gently moving breast.

Lovely Woman in the Lake, My Wife, My Love

Where you move
water *is* desire – desire *water*
and for me, a kind of liquid everywhereness
fluxed within contours
inner motions and the softened fulcrums of your sex
all flag and wind
is man
caught up, his architecture
aping strength
until the instant of forgetting
(a blood pulse in the drumming dark)
he would live for your body
like a soul possessed
reside within the incredible dominion of your flesh
thinking about being alive
and nothing else.

When We the Velocities of Wonder

When we the velocities of wonder
have slowed
like the pulse of sleepers
growing slack
in dreamless dark
an instant from the mind
lighter than the pulm of breath
that bumps leaf against leaf
what shall we worship then
if we should worship well
centred like a scream
within the shrinking zeroes of our fear
by making eyes
the pupil of the man
to hold with prophesies of stone
or make from these sweet finities of flesh
unwind their secrets from the bone?

The Sad Mathematics of Our Lives

At journey's end
after the muffled thud of car doors
when these children
are brought bundled in sleep and half sleep
hefted victims of the night
drugged in radio light
time smouldering in a dream
under stars
heartbroken by the logic of clocks
and the sad mathematics of our lives
we count our blessings.

Driving the Drumlin Road
by Jocelyn's at Dusk

The sun was wild once, wild as children
in these hills
humped now
like horses lying down
but colour falls asleep at dusk
and moonlight slides
like a lover's gentle hand
between the slips and drifts of shape ...
though here we may have been stuck
in this pot's-bottom of a world
busy at jobs we hate, bad marriages
where the noise of commerce
rattled its agitated monkey bars in the skull ...
now we float
as if the earth had given up her gravity
exchanged this multiplicity of cares
for silence and solitude
when the very quiet aromates the air
and heart settles
on its haunches to philosophize.

Fat Little Girl Singing in the Lake

Fat little girl
singing in the lake
her body like soft cake
in the watery absolutes that announce themselves
thundering unheard beneath her tiny voice
this small exquisite reed
of undistractable humanity.

Watching Dusk Fall in the Cottage Yard

We were watching
from the cottage yard
while darkness
smudged the blue distance like an oily thumb
then drifted in the close catalpa leaves
or etched the lilac
and tipped the weird mid-June bronze of its petals

while dusk slowly fuzzed the print of our books
gnats could safely drop then
like spies in the brown-as-river water cold coffee
or tick in the leaves and the high ditch grasses
like gentle rain
and hum in the smoky swarm like a choir in a distant church.

Just at that moment when cool first climbs the back of the hand
and tickles the arm hairs
we listened for one last breath
to where the lake
rolled its pebbles and mined the shore wash
for the final kiss-wet bits of pink.

Listening to Peacock Point
on a Summer Night

The rattle of dice on a game board
a lone mosquito humming like a lazy seamstress
in a dark room
the radio mumbling like a spy in the corner
an unattended kettle whistling in the kitchen
the clop clop clop of someone walking past on the road
the sound of girlish laughter
in the distant halo of store light
or a dog dragging his chain link by link
on the doghouse sill
then the settling huff of him lying down
the dim whip crack of a beach fire
snapping in dry wood
with the lake static beyond the cliff
where all night the quiet gods tune in the world
press an ear
against the short moonlit waves and listen.

By the Shore's Collapsing Waters
I am Bound

There are certain ways of making brevity seem brief.
Something you notice
in memory
some half-forgotten pain
some darkening flaw of love
like a gnat in the gloaming.
The long shadow you cast
standing in your lifelight.
The Kama sutra of many sleeps
where you curl and change
like the surface of the sea.

Waking on a Summer Morning

My mind begins its inner climb
with wasps fanning their wings
to cool the hive
within the walls of the house
beside our room
the wound of waking opens slow
with sound
these rainy windows veiled
like quiet weeping
of disappointed love
and light tinged with milky atmosphere
then drowsy as an egg
swishing the contours of a cold pan
I lift my head
to see how night has happened to the clock
and will not happen twice however much it's knocked.

Last Night it Thundered

Last night it thundered
and the whole sky rumbled above the cottage.
Windows shook in their watery casements
and trees lashed the house
like cruel captains too long at sea.
The boys came calling in fear
from their beds
their bodies still warm with interrupted sleep
while lightning snapped a yellow whip that
sizzled in the lake
like a scorched pan
gave a grey silver-nitrate glance at the heavens
vulgar with storm.
Rain thumped a thousand million urgent fists
against the shingles
then rushed for the gutters
and ran to the ditches beyond the blackened grass.

We lay in bed helpless with love
pressed for hours beneath iron-coloured night
till dawn undressed the dark
and rain uncurled its fingers
turned up its open palms and splashed
its lifeline in glistening threads
upon the road.

Queen Anne's Lace

Wild carrot flower
my grandmother's coffee-stained doily
with the whole field beyond
an ambitious nation of corn
you guard the fencerow
like a story.

"We were children once
upon a time   moving
a sure embroidery of moments
looking for a centre
by a cartoon-coloured sea."

Five Times Out of Nine

The sky was puking
in the storm drains
like a three-day drunk
and i had nothing to say
with my broken pulse
rabbit punching my temple
as if it were busy trying to be born

my shirt was red
as a murdered ghost
in the lamplight
wind was something being strangled
in the window casings
where curtains lifted their cheap hooker's shift
and showed me the night

and I'm always breathing
since the day i was conceived
my brain's been running
like a taxicab waiting for fare

my whole life spent trying to avoid anything terrible
before my body agrees with time
and dies
wondering which side of that moment
i will know
what it all meant

Neither a Leader Nor a Follower Be

for Don Linehan

Don tells me that
at night deer come down the hill
within the light cast from the house
as if they had books to read
soundless as calm dreams
foraging unwatched in windfalls
past the bent raspberry canes
above the La Have River
then he calls me from politics
to mark a nuthatch nursing a stump for beetles
and think how
sunlight is the kind of rose
God gives us all
so sooner or later someone will notice
and be amazed.

While the Night Pulls Up Its Roots

The night is black as tarnish
and you, my helpless son
manage your small collisions
in the opaque hall
where furniture lurks
the doorway shifts with shadow
moonstain whispers
in hardwood
and cobwebs caress like drifting gauze.
But you must suffer the briefest midnight journey
from the washroom
listening to your brother snoring
like torn fabric
with the house drowned in darkness
till you reach the ridiculous safety of your own bed
where you sleep again
while the night pulls up its roots
like sheep-nipped grass.

The Last Crucifixion of a Fly

The fly spends his last enthusiasm
beating a tantrum out
in the spider's web
that sticks to his wings
like a wedding veil
to a long inhale.

Then the widow Death drags her black thorax down
to where she spins
ticking in the skein
till the final unmendable blue buzz
is sealed
and suckable.

Fly's brothers droning over dog droppings in the yard
or walking the brown dent
of an apple bruise
or tiptoeing the soft obliteration of a dead sparrow
care not at all
that he is mummed
for dark Arachne's delectation.

Thus the world so loves her creatures
that she sends them
thimble chaliced as this blood-rich sacrifice
without remorse
though fly hums perplexed within the gauzy shroud
collapsing in her mandibles
like a martyred insect Christ.

Forgive the House that Made Him Wake

Tired old dog circles and circles
outside my father-in-law's bedroom door
before lying down
winding himself
like setting the hands of a clock for bed
adjusting every ache and twinge
then falling asleep the way summer darkness settles slowly
on a tree
or as a cloth drifts down upon an up-thrust knife
but if the house creaks only once
he'll leap up like a dozing sentry
to begin again
the hundred half circles he makes
like a compass on a dashboard
in a car, turning as it drifts
towards the bottom of a bottomless sea.

Saint Dog

Old Saint Dog
lies on the carpet
puffing
with the cancer
in his leg big as a sparrow
once or twice
death flashes
while Saint Dog dreams and he seems to know
that death comes
like the moon
and he runs to the light
through air as thick as water
always wondering why
he runs so slow.

Beyond Our Dogs

Death means
you are suddenly not old.
Startled by weightlessness
like a leaf in water
you carry the Cosmos.

You float
like laughter over a midnight campfire
and though you grew to hate the ache
of your arthritic joints
you hate them no longer
all the twinges gone
as the sweet and silly hungers of youth
return
but the body is something you've shucked
like sunlight
pouring through ice
the trivial particulars of life
have lost their fondness for your touch.

The way a curtain strains its wind-stirred hem
to life a Chesterfield
you've done and disappeared.
We've all too often caught this paradox
this disease of irony
beyond our dogs.

The Echo of Your Words Has Reached Me

> "Little man!" the mountain cried.
> "The echo of your words has reached me!
> Do you really think I can be contained
> in your song?
>
> *Inuit poet*

I Too Can Show the Way

Where would you lead me friend?
into what future
and from what past
and by what light guide
and for what purpose go
and to what end
and with what faith ...
for if I follow
where the hills are hard
and if I cross cruel rivers
on the way
stepping stone by stone
between the foams and froths
that break the water's voice
and if I look to see
who comes behind
by my example then
we share a path
and breathe to climb
and step against the slope
to see the valley's hard green ease
beyond a blind horizon's call
and if you'd named the dangers
one by one
and sent those glories free before
how then
to temper knowing
if I do not touch the stones the rivers touch
how then to look upon the map
and say
see there, we went together
    I too can show
the way.

first impressions from the air

Arctic open water
congealed with ice
waxy circles
of cold fat floating
in a bachelor kitchen
wet snow
cornflower blue
hallucinogenic frozen swirls
bannering under crystalline humps

the bay
a ram's fleece
cotted between the hills
the small town taxis under us
the harbour full of false bears
stone old
granite seals
and whales of seven hills

Inuit Graveyard, Iqaluit

sorrowful crosses mark
the death of the young
stuck like ships sunk to the gunnels in graves
meanwhile the oil-drum armour
of the harbour
rusts at the mouth of the same corroding stream
lacing through filthy red ice
the caribou ribs
curing like old men
crucified against houses
where on the roads
truck tires puff and growl
among the long-chained dogs gone mad

but who am I to wonder
though I do
at this sad biography of crosses

see how a mother
sinks her hands to the wrist
in permafrost
to embrace her lost child.

"I gave her a fox fur, and am ashamed"

in the filthy age
when the hunt was all
and seals scarce
and whales
like submarines of war
sought safer waters in the deeps beyond their boats
the char few; the caribou gone ...
an Inuit widow and her daughter
starved one winter
lost in a sculpt of frozen sleep

one man remembers
"I gave her a fox fur, and am ashamed"

and so he lived one long regret since then
weeping generously for himself
like an old eleemosynary rain

The Place Where Poets Pause

This is the place
where poets pause
to catch their wind
lean on their walking sticks
to consider the world
in the green meadow
among the moraines and eskers
beside the roaring river
beside the windy lake
after climbing the slip of scree
between snow-topped horns
breathing fast and hard
in the crack of glaciers
in the roar of waters
in the whispering of the world
above the Weasel.

This is the place
midst the dumb tongues of ice
where poets lie back on the lichen
while singing springs
carry their sputtering octaves
pool to pool
where buntings wing
and nest their naked squab
in down
and the fox-tracked sand
slides below a lemming stitch
and poets push their breath
to see the tiny gnarled willow
old red-fingered fellow clinging to his rock
to see the battle of blossoms
like wrestling daughters
careless of their party dresses.

Thor and Odin

Two great gods
stand on either side
of a rushing river
one regarding the other.
Will it be war
or thunder?
The ice roars and breaks
the peace
the gods respond
the one hurling boulders
the other stone still.

Meanwhile the valley flowers
the purple saxifrage
the arctic heather
the mullet and rhododendron
make tiny delicate whispers of wind
under the pompous booming mountains
in the stolid brown stare
of those two giants
they live like schoolgirls studying history
and giggling at the horrid faces
of dark leaders and dangerous heroes.

Dancing on Wind

i

Loaded
like a gold-rush mule
I trek
my pack
balanced and steady
in the thigh-deep glacial streams.
I ford the foaming rush:
my anthem, a cold scream
my flag, a blue snap of clear sky
my flower, the shivering saxifrage
my emblem, ice
my code, the quick cross
everything vein-coloured
my heart
slow as the plop of stones in water
my boots tied high
kicking together like a wish at my back
dancing on wind.

ii

glacial thunder
sounds its ceremonial gun
cracks and calves
cascading snow
falls in blind white sprays
fanning about the rock below

our footprints
recall us where we were
imagine us
where we have yet to go
sinking the size of a man
the depth of a day.

iii

walking the mountain moss
is like walking
on an old wet mattress
each step we sink
like bachelors in bed

iv

enthusiastic walkers
in good boots
we endure miserable weather
bad food, aching sleeps
barren land, long thirsts
glorious solitude
mountains and intimate sky
rivers and naked stones
to be where we are
exactly, resting, taking tea
sipping the land
in longing

v

the blistered writer
a spavined hiker
limps from camp to camp
with a broken pencil

Wise Rage

Somewhere on the tourist trail
on Baffin Island
a lone stone
perches like a granite egg
nesting high on an overhang of ice
where it tells
the patience of the ages.

Perhaps it will rest
awhile – eons
then fly at the sun
like David's brave desire
a small flaw of darkness
at the end of light.

Perhaps it will hang
on the air
after the last melting off
of gravity
set like a king's skull
in a crown of cloud.

Perhaps it will
fall and siege against falling
as it goes rumbling down
a cannon's dud
bumped from the muzzle to wreck the floor.

But there are fires in men
who live
on the blind gyre of earth
and their hearts burn holes in snow.

Mountain Avens

As if the hills had decided
not to save themselves
for their husbands.
As if they all loved
with the longing of lonely women
for famous men.
As if they had
but one desire
sighing open, tossing aside their foggy veils
in the pinking heat of a summer's dream.
As if they were
the wild daughters of foreign generals.
As if they posed
for their sugar daddies
and lay about lazy
seducing diamonds of dew
champagne poured in rainy slippers
one heel on the grey-haired heart
one on the white stone of a pillow.
Like a lady's permission
they will send the wind away
whistling.

Ten-Thousand-Year-Old Winter

Like Magna Carta ink
it flows from black-rock streams
an ancient democratic
death of kings
we touch our lips
to millennium
we drink away the ages
ten thousand centuries of ice
to chill our Adam's wine
we slake ourselves
on clean history
the ghosts of Frobisher and Penny
as new as mist
we seek a health
mulled before the middle ages
briefly came to Chaucer's life
we come to lichen rivers
where the snow recedes from stone
like the slow and heavy heart of gods
we drink as cavemen drank
when summer failed to come.

Older Men Speak of Food

young men talk of women; old men speak of food
          Russian proverb

We sit in the shelter
and fuss
rehydrating freeze-dried peas
so the green skins pop
stirring slowly
sipping, mumbling delectables
is the coffee hot? sweet?
strong? are the onions
crisp? is the sauce smooth?
thick?   ...oh, the dates!
Oh, the prunes!
gourmands of jerky
like a salty shoe tongue
delicious enough for here
and fromage
the dried apricot
folded like young loves remembered
by our mouths
we become nostalgic
our arms reach
like woody branches
for another taste of summer.

Midnight on Summit Lake
with Mount Bredalblik

the camera blinks
catches the five-blue Arctic night
clear as noon
from Inuksuk
to snow-swathed sublimation
of Bredalblik and beyond
high up where dreamers ski
the wide and brilliant runs of ice
the pushed-up
kettle of stone holds a lake below
for the prowling gods
saying, small man, small stone man
with your camera lens
like the popped monocle of a German duke
startled open by beauty

Never Again

the day before the day
we meant to walk
on the Penny Glacier
we'd climbed to the ice edge
and looked out over
the great white expanse
on the verge of that frozen world
having crossed
the Arctic Circle together
going north, pausing briefly for a photograph
at the formidable Inuksuk
placed there to measure the path
as we trekked past that geographic illusion
past that
along the Weasel
and we were rising slow
toward the stony shores
of Summit Lake
and the great promise of a grand tomorrow

we slept long and well
and woke to the earth
clothed in a white chimera of pogonip
that was chill and thick
as cold smoke
and we were fog-blind
from foot to fingers
lost in that tent-dampening light
with no memory of light left in the damp

and we were three days there
locked in that still weather
playing our flashlights through the veil
that when it lifted
let us go
in a rush of surrender
though it followed us
out, trailing down through the valley
with a slow crawl of vanishing stone
and I, like Orpheus
I, like Lot's salt-shaped wife
could not resist
looking back over my shoulder
followed as I was
by the ominous shadow of God

Starless and Blue at Midnight

Baffin skies
starless and blue at midnight
the moon has lost her clock
hiding among the mountains
the water colder for that hour
where the bunting flutters
and goes quiet

The Stone Bothy

Near Swartzenback Falls
a little stone bothy
sits lichen-thatched
weathering like peat smoke
but no one dwells there
in the barrens
only hare gnawing the black rock
where the lonely Inukshuk
herd caribou ghosts
in the snow

The Ravens of Baffin

the ravens of Baffin
circle and land
to scavenge their shadow
with clap-echoes joining in air
above concussive black wings
these second angels
visit like deathbed priests
and you can almost see
in their hungry eyes
how they wish we were dead
or dying.

All Summer in the Light

We've walked the land
of forgone darkness.
Into the night no children fear.
Into the moonless night
of disobedient and wishful stars
the absent galaxies
no northern/southern horoscope
to rule the birth of bears
marining their mouths
on the souls that slip in the sea
like seals of thaw.
And there, in that dreamer's deception
in the nicotine light
of false hours in the smalls of morning
the sun shines still
the sleeper's curse
he cannot cure with closing eyes
working his sheep and fences.

And if we age all evening
then wake to rub our beards
in disbelief
finding the smoother moments gone in sleep
the slow collapse of consciousness
into that
and breakfast on the boil, the porridge
bubbling like a wool sock half seen in water
the coffee cooling its own ghost
joining the larger fog
with the sun behind a mountain cloud
like butter in the buttermilk
come, let us rest our aching arms
and cease to stir the universe with looking.

A One-Beard Journey

We've made a one-beard journey
up and back
through the winding valley
of the Weasel River
going north then south
in this Arctic wilderness
this place of infinite solitude
and rugged beauty
so various and large
it seems to double wonder.

And I sit
enthroned upon a rock
under the sun
and a cotton-pharmacy of cloud
in the roar of water
by a broken indecisive bridge
yawning above the rapids
a double-dance step short of death
and I see
the tar-dashed face of the range
across a coil of streams
and I say
"I am here, Lord.
Do you see me
among the rhododendron?
I am the only flower here with hands."

Where Are You Now Cathy Jeanne?

Like a gunless soldier away from home
I've spent two weeks walking
these stony trails
sleeping on an ache of earth
like a hard-bellied lover
everything reminds me of you
the yellow clutch
of Arctic poppy
the mountain heather
the rhododendron
even the stones and snow
have their metaphor
      pure absence –
and the rainbow
arcing above the blue glacier
where our son stands
the best result of love
where two souls touch
among these merely crossing clouds.

Returning to Night

We are returning
to night
where darkness comes
upon a nod of roses.

An Almost Silent Drumming

Rumours of the Police

On our first night in Johannesburg
there is a sudden commotion
in the parking lot
just outside of the well-glassed restaurant
where we are with our calamari
and Windhock beer
simply beginning our visit.

And there is something
just beyond the circle of light
tossing its thin silk in a yellow drift
of its own description
just there by the car in question
sitting in shadow
like something sunk to the roof in brackish water
while five youths scatter
as the illuminating blue swirl
of the law arrives
and we watch it all
like cockroach scuttle
and one constable, his hands lamping the tree
becomes someone simply sweeping the dark
from the limbs of a larch.

And there is nothing there
nothing to satisfy or disappoint
nothing to drag by the leg.

And as we watch
the policemen go
and after in the slowing
those who have run away
return
to surround the little car
glancing up as if a kite were caught
and tearing its own cloth in the grief.

And so, our conversation
turns to intersections to avoid
to fear of guns
to why we must never stop at stoplights
to how a husband was shot in his home
to car jacking, to drugs
and the crime
of those in a hurry to be
'not poor'
'not homeless' 'not jobless'
'not without water' 'not
without food'   'not here!'
our conversation turns
in candle flame
and white wine flavour
and in the good cheer of linguine con mari
to where, outside the window
those city children
mill around that car in question
looking up
and wondering
what's up there in the branches?
how might it set us free?

The Orchard at the End of the Wind

Are you lost
in the orchard
at the end of the wind
where it finally dies
in a gasp of red-pit cherries
where it were as if to perish
among the plums
like a child's sleepy kiss gone sweet
or at the dying down of the day
in the brushing of boughs
bent in the buxom way of peaches
or like ladder shiver
and the shape
of a picker shifting her weight
outreaching at the last
aching instep of gentle
apple pluck?

Were you there that day
among the double bower
of winter jacaranda
on the rust-red boulevards
of *our* Pretoria
dreaming another fragrant summer
another purple night
in the smaller aromas
of an improving south?

Were you there
on the blue-gum journey?
Did you sojourn
for an hour
of shifting light
to watch the stone-fed egg
of an almost vanilla-coloured sun
slip down
an edge of sky
to an unknown ocean
into some dark harbour
& did you listen to my lesson
on fading
and the physics of photosynthesis
of etiolation
with the heliotrope yearning in you
leaning as would
the weary
as would the sad
as would the waterless
outer concern of my home's garden?

And if I think
how every history
has its Blood River
how every nation's delicate treachery
involves indelible memory
and the awful twin poisons of false hope and half-truth
will you not simply
rest with me then
in the still
at the rim of the well
and watch
how those fructifying lanterns
hang in the fullest slatternly girth of their heaviest season
and we will be
a parliament of breathing
& a goodness
we will send
        the weather on its way
to bless the Grey Lourie
tell his feathers
an artless engine's turning out to blush
the groves through growing
& we are here
to mark their suppuration
though they fail themselves
with one long
commencement of ineluctable falling.

Soweto and Souwesto

This is where
Soweto and Souwesto meet
this double palm
two men might hold in salutation
these human lifelines touching
like skin rivers
blending below the heart
where the sternum's echo flows
to a smaller drum
blue-dimpled like a water drop
upon each inner wrist.

I see this squatter slum
this smoken squalor
these stolen corrugations
wimpled in metallic rhythms of the sun
from under brilliant umbrae
through hundred-thousand small-roomed doors gone dark
with all the lethargy of want
aspiring for a better light.

I greet
these men and shape
the language of our snows at home
from one internal weather
where filigrees and fronds of frozen stars are falling
from the mind
as if upon the Speed
the Grand, the Thames
the blue St. Clair and all
with one ubiquitous hiss
of old December's heaven
in the whispering waterways of memory.

And we linger in the shade of talk
and I am ashamed to hear myself ...
I have no healing words
Souwesto and Soweto
seem such a simple sibilance apart
and yet
I'm fat with lexicons
for everything but this
the almost silent glossolalia of my heart
the single 's'
subsumes entire alphabets
Soweto and Souwesto
share this moment
in different blinks of time
while consonants lull great continents to sleep.

False Lions

The dog below the chair
dreaming
otherwise quiet dreams grows loud
in mocking the lions
as he moves.

Susan says of her Jaffa
not so very far
from the bushveld
where the great cats roam
& prey in prides of Africa
"Quiet, listen, do you
hear him?"
this tiny canine creature's breathing out
an atavistic slumber.

And yes
I've heard policeman's starlings
I've heard
the flattered crows
set guard against
such mimicry
and all the gulls
in chorus
at the train yards
accusing every jesting smoke
in swarms of flight.

But here
the little dog's
a better clown.

And Susan also told me then
of how a somnolent drunk
mistook himself
for danger dozing
on the floorboards of a car.
How game wardens warned
by his whereabouts
went still
and hushed the listeners
identified the feline lord's
proximity, so marked
by the low rumble
in one approximating throat.

"Do you hear the lions?"
they said.

And all the listeners laughing
jackal to jackal
to the last glottal
of this imitative sleeper's most sonorous work.

Sitting Poolside in Suburban
South Africa

I am here, friend
with my very own face
reflected in this fallen sky
neither as boneless dog
fabling out his loss
nor as the flowering ghost
of the drowned and beautiful boy
though the fragrant honeysuckle hangs its white
response upon that second fence
where it fails its own perfume
though it blooms and twins
and its green and purple foliage
suffers a wet desire in design.

I watch the facetating counter waves
of wind-stirred circles
and streaking opalescence
transparent anemones of breathing skies
the rippling physics of shivering machines
undulating all the lily float
of one blue and fascinating stillness
yearning to be still.

And here and there
Namaqua daisies promise themselves a life
to live when the rain comes
to the rockery
the leafless shimmer of trees
hold branches out in hope
above the braai
like a blessing of the dead year
in already fleshless hours.

And the low jasmine
and well-woven palm
where weaverbirds steal away and away
with tiny yellow rings
and weed-wild nameless things
all reach and spindly reach
but do not touch
the thing they reach for
the self-affirming perfect doppelganger
where only the foolish drown in joy.

Sudden Fascination

It came upon us
of a lazy Sunday –
the sudden fascination
of a fire (near distant)
first seen as slow smoke
and the curious scent of burn
followed fast
by yellow billows
and the hot-dry
ominous leap & crackle of burning grass
caught dying by the spruit
and then, almost leaping the walls
of these well-walled yards
as red heat seen
by the jagged saw-toothed spirit
of light and peril come.
Meanwhile, all along
the lethargy of waking dogs
all along
the sleepy insouciance of neighbours
half-heartedly looking out beyond their fences
with the odd klaxon
bleating and impatient with the drive.

But ah –
in the briefest whimsy of our fear
to feel the freedom and delight of something moving
in the day.

We'd steeped our tea.
Let's watch
and listen
then lift our tindered feet
on strangeness
like the blind.

Loneliness as an Art

I have
heard
how loneliness
as an art
of the spirit
might
show us truth.

Some of us
are such
solitary liars
our soul
becomes a breathless stranger
exhausted
by the company of one.

In the Belly of the Ndebele Village

And then there was John
the Ndebele carpenter
drunkenly showing us
the thousand-year-old grass-thatched village
the lovely lonely dung-washed floors
with their patterns
where women sat swirling their palms
to the right of their men
the Ndebele lords
above them on their benches
and we
with our own
slug-leafed histories
we see in them
the awful tribal misogyny
of other cultures
walking into the ever-growing western
architectures of contact and colour
we place the cruel female circumcisions
and the bigamy of men
with the father's cattle kraal
to measure wealth and deference
and the tyranny of the dead ...

This tall and gentle thatcher
John, with laughing eyes
has eight children and two wives
and is himself
the son of fathers
himself a man of men
though he wears a bowling shirt
and has a tongue
that breaks our language
as one would be humbled by a half-known song.
Yet he's braceleted about by time
come cut away before him
 like the precious water grasses
of an ever-making mat.

Taken

In the mind of the lion
the entire floor of available earth
is a banquet.

It matters not
whether we are poets
or pious strangers.
She will take us as a huntress
at our prayers
and make a foolish martyrdom
of grace.
The child, her mother
the silly simpering debutante
pausing at the virtue
of a water face
adjusting her hips
to tease her gait
and make an envious vanity
of walking watched ...
There is no poverty
so penurious the lioness will not fell it
no wealth
she'll pass.
She'll humble all her hungers
to one belief of beggars
under a glorious insouciance of stars.

And so too, at home in Canada
the rogue black bear
stole one entire life
athletic and alone
distracted by an inner arrogance
a single rattle of the spine
at the softness of the nape
and she was gone
to puzzle out her place
among the running dead.

And here's the same
among the predatory perils of this dark continent
two hapless tourists
were simply *taken*
as it is with smoke by wind
as it is
with a name unspeakable
it cries with this final unrequited sob
of man to God.

Automatic Dogs

Johannesburg, White Suburbs, August 2000

All along
the willing prison of the street
the automatic dogs
bark on and off
to mark the passing
of a man
this gated village grown so noisy
cell by cell and wall by wall
this rise and fall
of jail-yard echoes
thrilled to staggers
voice to voice
how loud the fences
how high
and low an emptying out
of sound
the throaty toughs
the yappy whelps
even the silent
yield up unhealthy fits of troubled breath
as heel toe passers by
excite and sooth
as if
consuming volumes pitched their best and worst
by one long windy vowel
hoofing down the hills.

And in the distance
meanwhile and far away
entire canine nations
burn down dog dictionaries
reducing them to one valiant and futile
long lament
because where dogs are talking
everyone listens.
While dogs are talking
pedestrians set nervous watches on the locks.

I Saw Them Walking in the Morning,
I Saw Them Walking in the Night

I was sitting
in the garden by a pool
in suburban Johannesburg
when an English schoolboy
from beyond the razor wire
and broken-glass wall
came in through the locked-after-him gate
bringing a white pail
of brackish water
dipped for me out of the costal
waves of the Indian Ocean
off the shores of South Africa
where my great aunt Ida spent her final days
dying the year of my birth
eleven full months before I was born
and he brought it here
by way of a one-day round trip
to Durban
and the lad was a young teen
an Anglo prig
full of racist talk
typical of his class
and though I cringed at the ugliness of that
still, I removed my right shoe
and dipped my grateful Canadian toes
into the briny clarity
my ankles white as milk shine to the sock top
and I know he thought me a fool
to feel the trill
where my open heart
met the small circle of

that wet circumference rising
a cool elixir of portable light
liquefying my pale flesh
with the tidal ablution
of that far-away place
my anklebone becoming
moon blessed, a polished stone
time-deepened and dream washed

meanwhile the narrow-templed English schoolboy
went on and on as though he spoke with the wise palaver
of the worldly traveler
he yawped and yapped
about the servile ingratitude
of lazy cooks and feckless workers
all those arrive-in-the-morning
leave-after-dark
peons who did not know their place
though they laboured and were bird-busy
in his father's yard and his mother's kitchen
toiling and lolling at the behest of
the good will of their masters
living in this world he wears
as flag and border
crest and crown

and I saw them walking in the morning
I saw them walking in the night

and I wonder at the failure of this young boy's shadow
gilded by an edge of darkness that fails to see the light

Rumpy Pumpy

What can I say, first
we saw two ducks breeding
at the Johannesburg zoo
the drake
flacking at a whitewashed angle
tossing his brush
in a brief and painterly perfection
in the grass.
Meanwhile three girls
giggling behind their hands nearby
knowing nothing about this
but the slightly silly
feathering sidelong glance
of both the mounted
and the mountee
engaged in something so seemingly ridiculous
it made them laugh.

Next day
in among the dry rustle
of the brush thorns
an ostrich
stopped herself, hunkered down and flapped away
her pheromones
drawing the black-winged male
who came dashing at her
with the long-legged yarding
of his own goofy desire.
And there, at dawn, in Africa
they flooded the morning
with flagrant big-winged motion
as he fertilized her monumental eggs.

We watchers
joked about *rumpy pumpy*
for days
flapping our arms to mock
an animal concupiscence
as with a strange intensity
of birds
the Lourie, the hornbills
the crimson-breasted beauties
set watches
wondering when we might begin
our brave display.

Dark City

This most recent squattery
on the rim of Johannesburg
is dark at the gathering hour
because there are no electric lights.
The night gone blind
goes deeper in the earth
takes root
and squanders every candle
to a scorch of wicks
like a bristled singe of winter grass.
And here
the smoke crawls downward
becomes a burning serpent
with lightless lungs
a weighty overuse of air
a flung-down fleecen thing
so shorn to one wide smothering
it seems
the brazier is choked within
with unused coal
the paraffin exhausted on its match
and there
beside the road entire
the ditch is moled away
to hold cold fire in
along a dying edge.

A dozen moneyless languages
drift up
to smudge the windless wing
while we are passing
when and where
an evil eye is shut
on redness, warning
though heat and tinder blink
and leap the road
they do not catch
the watching
for failure of attention
to the sliding link
the slipping scale
our headlights
cast a brilliant hope
that cannot see ahead.

Refusing the Dark

We are arriving at night
near Mount Pilansberg
in South Africa
at an hour
when fire best remembers what it is
and refuses the dark
as all along a red line of controlled burning
we witness
that brilliant crimson creature
crawling
the illuminated memory of itself
so we see where it is
in the countervail of shadowless light
making a windless climb
in the loud heart.

Next day
we are cozened by snow-patches of
almost extinguished ash
and a true-black earth
where the green shoots push the carbon scorch
as a blunt thread might test the needle's eye
in the blur and fray of an old woman's work.

And the zebras come to graze
like chain gangs
they drop their muzzles
and taste
the ancient and forgetful thing
because where winter's going
we must follow into spring.

My African Stone

As light wears down this stone
the sun's up somewhere else
rubbing fire on the rim of things renewed
and even while
the songbirds sing
the night along its lassitude
with the widow's bolt of heaven
come to weeds
and mourning's done with woe
the joyful rock
we ride upon
lifts colour and erodes to brilliance
all its shadow-measured minerals.

Meanwhile I steal for home
this lamp-bright garden paperweight
which on my desk
is but a planet's fraction of true memory –
though winds may come
it holds the blotter
like a mending hand.
And if it trust me
might recall
the lengthening illusion back to breath
when Adam was but dust
and mothering crowned our skulls
with wonder.

An All, Most Silent
Nelson Mandela and the Inuit − Goose Bay, Labrador

At an airport runway
his small jet refueling for further flight
the great emancipator
from South Africa, Nelson Mandela
walking the tarmac
saw through the fence
how twenty Inuit youth
had come to watch and say farewell
at Goose Bay, Labrador
north of the Arctic Circle
in the chill air.
And he thought
how small the planet
how living on the roof of the world
these the people
had come to wish away the hero
they'd seen released
from jail
on the southern tip of Africa.

And there they were
these two indigenous races
the adolescent Eskimo
shouting "viva ANC"
and the venerable Thembu
born on the banks of the Mbashe River
the lawyer from Witwatersrand
the lion among the people of the seal
come from the land of green winters
to briefly walk the permafrost
where ten-thousand-year old ice

crawled backwards
from great V's of rock
with a permanent white heaviness
rumbling like hungry bear gut
under an all-surrounding sky.

And I wonder too
what God must think of us
as in the slow centuries
evolving light eats at the shadow
which though it darkens down, returns
and as an aging shade grows thin
it yet repeats itself by shrunken darkness
blackened down like tarnish on old silver
while what the elderly learn
is lost and must be learned again.

An Afterness

I hear
an almost silent drumming
of this human heart
and know
it is my own.

And then
between the quickening
and the slowing
of sleep
between the rising
and lulling
of that excited inner touch
with all the thump
and thrum
of something captured
in the dark
I'm lost
between
the fearing of the known
and unknown ecstasies of life
as at the end of every
measuring
the stilling pulse
will seek and find and soothe so lovingly
the long lacunae of an afterness.

The Mission of Angels

The Mission of Angels

"silence is then a good equipment"
                       Pere Le Jeune   *Jesuit Relations, 1637*

What of a people silenced by time
like chastened children
sitting in Sunday chairs
the deeper the gravity the less they tell
in the ossuary where Neutrals lie
in among catlinite beads
banged kettle brass, hammer stones
conch-shell pendants and gorgets
these people of braceleted bones
this blacken-faced feast of dead souls
lost-tongued and quiet
though kitchen dumps of mud-cat spines
and carp and bass-ribbed
middens, ash beds to the age
shout and claw the air
tangled in plough blades like maple roots
cut into shares.
And that village there
below the city
in ripples of clay
where Mud Creek and Fairchild meet
and mix their waters
like rich conversation
of intelligent rooms where philosophers live
that place once called *Kandoucho*
All Saints Village
in Attawandaron tongue
that place called *Notre Dame des Anges*
by the friars of the Recollect

Joseph de la Roche Daillon
the scoundrel Étienne Brûlé
the mapmaker Sanson
and all the other
obliterated travelers of time.

Voltaire said
history is a trick the living play on the dead
and so the Neutral Nation
misnamed by Champlain
expires and is subsumed
and so the transitory journeying
of Gallic voices
have wintered in a siege of snow on pine
have summered
in birdcall grieving the ghost of oak
have sung their vaporous songs in smoky branches
basswood, ash, beech, elm
walnut, maple, alder, and all
the Latin lamentation
of the wind's declension ululating loss.

And my city, my brave home
my Brant's Ford
plays this trick on the dead
if they have not lived in ink
they have not died in time
their bones lying together
in graves
like branches come to dust
though we carry their ghosts on our breath
like smoke.

*In a Language
with No Word for Horses*

In a Language with No Word for Horses

the Hochalaga *savages*
coped with the French
carriage and horse
by speaking of *cabins pulled by moose*
where they ran
on mud rivers
lain upon the wilderness
village to village
with Champlain's vision
as he said "spoiled by mountains"

Sometimes it seems we look
and see the world.
Sometimes we speak
to name the snow
accumulating against a door
that will not open
either way.

A Dwindling Down of Dwellers

Between the coming of Cartier and the coming of Champlain
the Hachalaga natives were all dead and gone.
For fifty years their village lay abandoned
a dwindling down of dwellers
carried off by sickness
though the world was a soundless prayer of moaning
in the large and empty cathedral
of wilderness woods
howling ghost wolves of long winters
while the snow lay its altar cloth
on table rock
and the lakes and rivers
groaned with spring
with the tectonic heave
of earth in ice
at war with itself
in a shift of nations.

And why regret the ocean's grieving ships?
Why lament the grandiose weather of stars?
When each small life
blinks its soul to signal God
as to the loneliness of dying
under branches clicking like the death-kick of a deer
brought down
and eaten by time.
There's your mercy. There's your worship.
May as well bay at the moon
and pull your shores asea
and pray French boats be flung by rivers to the sky
like beetles riding ribbons
in the wind.

The Children of Brouage

As one of the children
of Brouage, Champlain knew
terror, hunger, hardship
war and the sight of death
this litany of suffering by the sea
this list, this inventory
of human hurts rolling the water
against a tower's base
wore away an early life
and Samuel as a prophet sang
devotions to sorrow
with the stations of pain gone dumb
in a Catholic house
and he soldiered well
and he sailed and sketched
and wrote devoutly
of the Quetzal bird
which never comes to earth
but flies until it falls
footless sparrow
and is dead
and *there be dragons* in Mexico
hovering over silver slaves and an Inquisition
too cruel to endure

and home, he made
barefoot pilgrimage
to the church on the cliff
overlooking the port of Honfleur
and he set sail
with heart a suspended anchor
let drift his soul
for the shores of Canada.

The Lengthened Shadow of One Man

In the longitude and latitude of life
he was
soldier, sailor, mariner, linguist
father of New France
husband, master, carpenter
devoted son of the church
explorer, cartographer, general
farmer, artist, author
hunter, naturalist
scientist, astronomer
so the lengthening shadow of one man
like ink spilled upon a map
sinks into the land
and shades the green forever.

The Angels of the Self

Champlain sailed from France to Tadoussac
from there to Cathay in a ship of air
through wild and forbidden forests
to green and pleasant inland islands
from the world beyond the rapids
to the great salt sea
from Lachine west
to where the sun
follows a dream of itself
as life flows into light
leaving a trail of darkness
with the fading
shadow wetness of a river tide
and as with the flight
and settlement of gulls
upon the savage breast of earth
the angels of the self rise
to set and swell against the wind
like the waving handkerchiefs of kings.

The Six-month Winter of Isle Ste. Croix

Locked on the island
by a jail of ice
grinding its gears of river
in shot-up sections
of frozen shale held white
like beasts in fear
before they fell in cold retreat
the seventy-nine listened to life
breathing off in timber houses, set
among phantom winds of winter
whistling weird melodies
of snow that lay on darkness
like salt on meat.

And they died
pulling their teeth from their mouths
as painless losses to the jaw
like plucking shells
from mud.

And Champlain
dissected the dead to seek the source
of demise, after they slipped into apathy and despair
with the brackish mood
of eternal night upon water
anchored to their beds
by the body's climate gone hoar
and the heart's small shallop
loosing its pull on the soul
the sun sinking in the west
like a blood pudding.

The Dragons of Beyond the Known

the draconologie of unknown seas
with the wing span
of fire clouds
these dragons (among angels)
shaking their scales
like the noble mail of unhorsed
river fish
thrashing in shallows
spawning in rocks
drying in droughty mud
with a sigh of gills
like small doors
gone shut on silence
and sadness.
These huge angry flights
of ill intent
engulfed in self-made
smoke of rage
seem the edge of storms
the rolling darkened nimbus
of a coming rain
the living weather
where distant water
jumps and rolls
and rears its crest
of drowning wind
with a roil of sailors
lost and corking their souls
with questing hands
catching a clutch of heaven's cloth
before they go

mouthing water
not even the granite statues stony gulp of earth
can claim
such filling up.
Oh, the dragons of beyond the known
to the water serpents
of the dark Magog
we have such monsters
in the mind
they blind us flying
while we sleep.

Knives Over Water

June 9th, 1610, Samuel de Champlain, in the company of Algonquin warriors, defeated the Iroquois in battle at the mouth of the Richelieu River in Quebec. The Iroquois vanquished the French in a second incursion where Champlain himself was wounded.

He came through the woods
shining like a fish
his helmet – a silver lily
his breastplate – a stove
he carried the long blast
of his blunderbuss
like the announcing brash of arriving kings
and armed against courage
armed against the local art of war
he raised death to his shoulder
and aimed the red miasma at the trees
so thunder in the powder sent the shot
to shatter ribs
to stop the heart of foes
to break the ranks of Iroquois
and see them bent down before him
like sow-crushed grass.
He won the day
beyond where the palisade
sank its fangs in the underjaw
of the earth at the river's mouth.
But losers learn
how to loathe a weapon met
already old the second time it's used
how a helmet
tossing among branches
comes away spotty with weather
and wounded by the rusty rain
and all the bloody iron of the world
where lost blades go dull
in the brief advantage
of knives over water.

A Shameless Girl,
A Handsome Stranger

He took the sun
to find his place
by astrolabe
from Matchedash where
he refused upon the fertile earth
the kindness of young girls
where he bedded on the ground
and spent the night with fleas.

June 10th, 1613

June 10th, 1613, Champlain lost his astrolabe near what is now Cobden, Ontario. His astrolabe was found two hundred and fifty four years later by a farmer and sold to an American because the finder thought it worthless.

Leaving behind ships at harbour rocking their masts
like the crooked crosses
of inlet graves
cocked in stone
the Dom de Dieu
had taken route in ocean rivers
where they were deep and wide
with all the moonlit wisdom of enlightened waters
arriving in New France and then
passing
escarpments with the great ice carving
a valley before them
scouring down shale
to the soft green nap of the earth
where land sleeps
while humus rolls away the ages
leading to where the nascence of nature
rediscovers itself in the spring
from the edge of thaw
to the verdant verge of summer
like a poem inhabiting itself inching at discovery.

Here the astrolabes of Europe
carried the men who carried them
fixed against heaven
lost in centuries of light set against our births
and in the woods
two hundred and a half and four years since
the navigator's instrument

sat siting Paris and the slow stars
sinking through the lassitude of time
like a burning hinge
with Champlain's eye

the triple blue of water sky
where the rete of the mind
and the sun-brass rete
converged in the farmer-found dross of the glebe
sold off
as a worthless thing.

Time and Ptarmigan

and I think of Champlain
going lost in the new-world woods
discharging his blunderbuss
like the cough of carried fire
or following the trail
of strange game
a beautiful bird
hallucinating ahead of him
parrot-beaked, hen-sized
red-headed, yellow-bodied
blue-winged, leading him
deep into the woodsy beast
so he circled
in the *dense macabre*
tethered to the large unmapped
moments we live
in unfamiliar times.

Hélèn in Canada

she had barely the beginnings
of broken beauty
when this child bride Hélèn Boullé
daughter of bourgeoisie
was contracted in marriage
to the great Champlain
who would not consummate
in winter's bed
who brought his new wife
gifts of quill and leather
who carried her hopes abroad
until she'd spent
four years in misery
suffering the snows of colony
and then the Catholic convent
took her in
and he went his gouty way
under the ache
of a sailor's cross
and she, with a locket mirror
between her breasts
lived that time cloistered in the wilds
saying, "I keep you there because I love you so"
to show the happy faces
flashing back.

The Poet Lescarbot

the blue-boat poet Marc Lescarbot
in his long seaweed beard
posing as Poseidon in his blue robe
came aside the pinnace
reciting glory
his trident like a farmer's fork
thrust three-pronged
into blue heaven, praising
Poutrincourt and Champlain
predicting Acadie
and New France's future
as a map might wish it
with the creeping stain of colonies
like Spanish wine
spilled on linen.

By What Was He Betrayed

By water was he drowned.
By the one long drink
of sinking
through heaven's looking glass
like a heavy trunk of guns
his boats
foundered and breaking
in wooden waves
against the stony jaws of shore.

By the bush
was he lost
in the wild tangle
of primordial dark
tethered by madness
to the map-less snapping
of branches.

By weather
and December's scurvy winds
was he starved
in the howling hearth of winter
while bleached rivers
foamed beneath his feet
in jagged shivers
of wet glass.

By land
too hard for graves
refusing the dead
for frozen months
the black-mouthed corpses
ate the night
until first thaw
wounded earth open at the heel.

By war and trade.
By axe and arrow.
By arquebus and cross.
By tongues and women's wants.
By all the sons of milk
and grace and gold.
By king and court.
By time and its every measure
with the brittle etiolating
of the world
rattling south.

By all beasts and birds.
By all the weird
caterwauls of the new world
where it shat at his feet
or in wide
guano swaths of gulls on granite.
By all the poisons
slithering off rock
and by the tri-lobed oils
and green ointments
of enemy shade
and

by friends
who under the same flag
who with a shared faith
who with a single voice
and one duty
unlocked their hearts
to mutiny and treason
became the treacherous blood drums
we die by:
Duval – his head impaled upon a spike
at Quebec
Brulé – boiled alive by Hurons
and he – Champlain
stricken by paralysis and put to bed
with life a stolen river
flowing on without him.

The Startled Blue Flowers of Light

An ocean away
he entered the nave of the Christ child
and slowly sank into death
after the cannon boom had brought
Christmas day to 1635
after the te deum laudamus
was sung at midnight mass
he surrendered the ghost
where it clung in the world
and he was styled
Father of New France
pious, celibate, pure
as the first unshriven snows
found upon the earth
in hills lashed like a Jesuit's back
by the penance of low branches
and the holy water running
where winter had failed the creeks.
And he was styled
the Cardinal's Lieutenant
and his will bequeathed
a clearing called *Plains of Abraham*
where the trees were felled
like soldiers in the clout of nations
on old land, he died
with the tremors of an alien flag
in unfamiliar winds the colour of water and blood.
Oh, the shivering cloth.
Oh, the startled blue flowers of light.

The Bones on Rue Buade

Beneath the city streets
the bones under Rue Buade
swim the earth
like a broken ship
from the long thigh
to the puzzle of the foot
from the metatarsals of the hand
to the skull unhinged
like anatomy class
gone to clay
the mandible tongueless
as a doll
and yet, Champlain might hear
the seeking hearts of priests pounding
from where he perished
to the parish grave, in epochs
to the endless lap of water
shore to shore
with the cross he made unmarked
upon the breast of seas
a score of time and nine
and stood on stone
as statues do
or drew himself a shirt of arrows
at a wooden wall
the northern palisades
he stormed
and failed to breach.
Oh, walk the eyes of children
walk the thoughts of men
walk the dreams of living sleepers
walk against the morphia
of horses clopping
in modern style.
We are more than quaint.
Walk us home.

Though Their Joined Hearts Drummed like Larks

Étienne Brûlé

Born about 1591, at Champigny-sur-Marne (near Paris), Brûlé arrived in North America as Champlain's servant. He was 16 at the time, and soon became Champlain's most trusted scout and pathfinder.

Two years later Champlain agreed to let him live among the Algonquins, a First Nations people, to learn their customs and languages. Brûlé traveled widely and most authorities agreed he was probably the first European to see most of the Great Lakes.

He was captured and tortured once by the Senecas, but survived, and became an interpreter among tribes as well as for the French.

When Brûlé was 33, a Récollet friar named Sagard denounced him to Champlain for what the friar felt were loose morals. When he was 38, Brûlé guided the English vessels that captured Quebec, sending Champlain and most of his little colony back to France.

Brûlé remained among the Hurons, and died, possibly in a quarrel, before Champlain returned four years later.

"silence is then a good equipment"

Père Le Jeune
Jesuit Relations, 1637

From the Mouth of the Humber

1618

From the mouth of the Humber
through Humber Bay
across the lake
to the Falls
riding a bucking bark
curved like a catalpa pod
in the womb of waters
Étienne Brûlé is clicking his tongue
to learn the savage words
the woods had heard.
For the trees knew their names
and the rivers
lingualated their shores
like the thirsty lap of dogs
while stags stood
like ten-point branches
bucking their racks
in the cool black shimmer
of a forest pond seeing themselves
as themselves
and the fowl flew above
and about
hovering wide-winged northern swan
singing of France.

The Intimacy of Canoe

Brûlé feels it move
in the smooth cut
in the slim groove
while the river
seeks itself further on
always, further on
chasing its own image
mistaking itself for sky
dropped shade, moonlight
the second man, each and every insubstantial twin
the trees in green groves, shore grass
the seen
bed in shallows
the unseen silt.
Deep below the level of light
where it dreams
with the heaviness of drugged sleep
too far beneath
impossible memory   the mind
goes on without us.

From Within the Yellow Engine of an Egg

i

Brûlé, you're an ant on a leaf.
You feel the river
beneath your boat skin
flowing like a lover's life
leg locked
you kneel and pray with your paddle
sojourn and journey
grass bent in the big surround
of water, earth and sky
with wind,--the breath of God
saying stay to the trees
stay to the rippling afterthought
of motion and moment
stay to the swirling up and settling back
of feathers blown away from birds
as if there were poems
written on the air
as if you were reading the silence
within the yellow engine of an egg.

ii

You carry the long craft
inverted
cutting the green portage above your head
the weight of heaven's sorrow
on your shoulders, lightly listening
to the echo-claw of branches
like widows scratching at a casket.
You stumble   strongly
past an angry stretch of river
to find peaceful water
further on
where stones blush to be touched
and your shadow
casts itself
to catch the mouths
of fishes.
Hungry for that kind of darkness
you chase the evening, steering
between birth and its
left-handed twin.

iii

Lake after lake subdued
each creek stretching out aft as if
the once familiar limbs of trees you climbed
as a lad
had newly fallen to the earth
and you walk the shade
of palpitating shadows
the shaken leaf closed up
darkness grown
over darkness

you fly by strength of mind
and map by jack-pine memory
by cedar-scent recall
by root tangle
and resting place
by struck fire
by summer's shrill singing
and the drifting off of sparks
learning how the night
might settle its bargain with the day
by the gambling off of stars.

iv

You enter the wildness
as the dead might enter a grave.
You've been sent that way by a still heart
locked like a clock in a trunk.
Under the black robes'
halo of darkness
you see circling their shoes
like the dropping of holes
that cannot be held in heaven.
Those shadow holes will have no third dimension.
Unlike the holes that let you look
into the weft and circumstance
of water
as wells will
seeing yourself and nothing else
beyond, because the light in your eyes
and the light in your life
are not the same.

V

You become so strong
you could almost
lift above your head
the Catholic blear of black and brown night sky
as a woman might pluck a wet garment from the water.
You can carry your own
troubles
like wind and weather
do the slant of rain.

And though you are hated
for deep desire
in the cock
with its failure to complete the hand
and its brief invasion
where darkness melts against darkness
and pleasure mends
the dimming down of differences
skin to skin.

And you learned their tongue
the language of their land
the love of their women
and the river remembers your weight
and the lake the slip of your craft.

A Priest Sees Étienne Brûlé and a Native Woman in the Night

i

Plunging his oar in her water lily womb
she rocks her hips like a still canoe
between her doe-brown thighs
and then her fever breaks and breaks again
as with the tug of a fish
pulling him into the deep-mud beauty
of her belly below the pond
his full weight sinking in that wet circumference
as she holds him
to that moment without movement
and he pulses like a cut snake
and she breathes out fear
while they are fastened.

ii

Brûlé has been kissing
the sailor's daughter
with his French mouth
to that second silence.

He has been
tucking the sea
in its shell
with his walking hand
sinking its cuticle moon
to the joint
to measure the tide.

She is not seeking a husband in him
nor is he wiving
though their joined hearts
drum like larks
shamming for strangers
too close the nest.

iii

The trees are not the only priests
who disapprove fleshly pleasure.
The rivers too
have gone as stiff as glass
and the lakes
have turned to jagged shores of stone
like giant jaws
slain against the sand
and heaven is one huge cold blue eye
gone blind with age.

Who can hide
when the birch is sweeping its white cane
in the wind
and the maple
creaks like a ship.

Then the tongue
learns to fuse to the wild
like a weed on a grave
with its roots
in the mouth of the dead.

Étienne Brûlé's Reply to the Priests

I am
an arrow
in a perfect wound.
You must draw me slowly
from my work.
Where the fawn falls
the hind
shivers her hip
while the sugar maple clicks
its buck rack
in the wind of winter stars
and rivers rut their ice.
If you nail my hands
like shingles
my feet like dowels and doves
I'll be thy holy house
and when the grape is cold
I'll mull the wine
and share the flesh
and be the kind of cannibal
who builds a church
of bones.

Father Joseph De La Roch Daillon's Journeys Among the Neutrals, 1627

i

I'm where Brûlé went before me
under the sheltering stars
five nights in the woods
lifting our eyes to the heavens
we sank with the land to our backs
for bed
into the huge paradise of darkness
with only the weight
of ourselves for mass
lying head to toe
citizens of night
while the heart went on
building its soft temple
out of dreams and bone.

ii

"I remark that in all this country
I met no humpback,
one-eyed
or deformed persons."

iii

The Algonquians tell the Neutrals
I am a sorcerer.
That I have
tainted the air
and poisoned many.
That I am Atatanite
:one who performs
sortileges.
That I intend to torch
their villages.
That I come
from a rude, sad, melancholy
race of long-tailed people
who live on snakes
who eat thunder
and marry one-breasted
cyclops-nippled women
who whelp like dogs
five or six to a litter.
And so one of them
knocked me down with a blow
while another
took an axe
and tried my skull
with a missing sweep
but failing that
they stole all
:breviary, compass, desk
blankets, bag of trifles
knives, needles, awls...
and so we were left goodless
in the beauty of God.

iv

The Neutral land is the best
and mildest I have seen.
Large and beautiful
with shallow-snowed winters
early melts and easy waters
a plentiful variety of game
both beast and bird
fruitful waters and bountiful earth
abundant and leading to laziness.

The children are bright
naked and disheveled
the men, given to hunt and war
the women
seem dissolute and shameless
immodest and lewd
giving their bodies over
freely to the wicked pleasures.

And yet
they sign the cross
to the grace of God
and glory of Christ.

V

I know I've failed my God
but the rumours of my martyrdom
have gone before me
like the sun that bleeds upon the water
bringing on the dusk
and then the dark
and so, I return
leaving the south in the spring
the lake gone blue behind me
like the slowing of the dead.

Sad Song

Champlain was shocked:

Étienne Brûlé
among the gleeful British thieves
that sorrowful July in 1629
the fleur-de-lye came down
at garrison Quebec
in the musket volley
and the ship's salute
of petty Treason
the blue French voices
wove within the red
like a sad song sung
beside a river.

Brûlé, you have lost your honour
wherever you go
men will point at you with scorn.
Better to die
than live on
in the world.
Whatever happens
you will always have
a worm
on your tongue.

The Cannibal Coffin
1633

...a fire was quickly lighted. Each savage took a flaming brand and burned the naked wretch. Boiling water worsened his pain. His nails were torn away, and fire applied to his privates. He was scalped and hot gum poured on his bleeding skull. The Bear Clan of the Huron of Penitanguishiene Bay, among whom he had lived for twenty-three years, pierced his arms at the wrist and tore sinews free. Ositsio, his former lover, climbing the stones to the torture tree, cried, "He is mine. He is mine. I will kill him." And she crushed his head with a blow.

Étienne Brûlé's body entered
the cannibal coffin
of human mouths
his hips of fire fed the village
his arms a long delight
to dogs
his belly rendered
with a greasy pottage.
His was the fate of a pole-axed heart
palpitating like a living clock
in the human hand.

Étienne Brûlé
walks home a dead man
dreaming
while his soul leaks off the meat like smoke.

After His Death

I saw the spot where poor Étienne Brûlé was barbarously and treacherously murdered, which made me think that perhaps some day they might treat me the same manner, and to desire least that it might be while we were earnestly seeking the glory of the Lord.
                Father Jean de Brébeuf, 1634

The Bear Clan addresses Brébeuf:

Father, might we dig up the bones of Brûlé
for they haunt us
in death.
Our village
is dying from plague.
Our kettle
is broken.
His sister
is cursing our smoke.
We suffer
the sickness of guilt.
We've burned
the longhouse of our kin
yet the ghost of that fire
has shaped itself
in a belching sky.
Save us
Father...

  and so, Brébeuf
gave permission
to the feast of dead souls...
though Brûlé
remained in his smother of earth
by the Bay.

And Brébeuf burned like the smoky
exhale of a wintering word...

Walking on an Ocean Beach at Dawn

The sun is at the rim of the world
where the blue
comes bannering free
both water and sky
like the run of a knife in a bolt of silk.

I walk among
the backward dash of crabs
while the toiling wash of the tide
approaches and retreats
the moon-slave achieving her last few inches of strand.

I walk the shore sand
seeking that bone-white second sea
replicating the winds of the world
in the valves of its shell
the small ghost ocean
carried by conches to the ear.

There in that grand eternal
clock of water and weather
I hear ships and the wheel of stars
for all that have sailed
and all that have sunk
to the weeds on a stone
to the beards of the drowned, gone green.

Bright Red Apples of the Dead

This Morning, My Father

the morning my father died
I was
walking the thousand miles
in his direction
under empty blue *wherein*

the sun came out like shirtstain
yellowed in the sleeve by sweat marks
to such a sadness
coloured in the cloth by cotton azure

and it was
so tough tempered
it soaked the earth
to a difficult green

while even the grass was straining to shade
against the loss of darkness
even I was locked in starwant
as I went
bronzing towards the sea
and sank to the chin
in south swell
as if I were rising
even the palms preferred an upturn
to the truth of whitened moonlight
even the shell hush
of bravery breaking

and I breathed to the fear fill
floating my heart
like a dozen still-breasted horses
drumming the sand and lashing the surf
in the splash line
of a far horizon

Newspaper Photograph of My Father Dangling His Feet off the Deck of the Lifeguard Tower on Carpinteria Beach, California, New Year's Day, 2003

This man who cannot swim
it seems is guarding the winter beach
he dangles his legs
from the tower dock
looking west to the ocean
his arms folded
against the shallow roar
of the sounding surf
with that catch-breath sand arranging itself
on ever-sputtering shores of time ...

I have never seen him
so much as damp-to-the-knee
though I've watched him once ankle blue
in the lake at home
in waves that barely wash the feet
walking among shells and pebbles
and warn-smooth bottle glass
with his pant legs rolled
like a tailor's last intention
in the clam-tide
that sucks the foaming stone

I do not think
I've ever seen him wade
nor let the water
scruple to the shin
how paper-white those calves
how heron thin

at home this man is landlocked
yet here he sits
in wind that fans his collar
like a pair of ancient gills

When You're Down on Your Knees in a Field Called Forever

The last time Ernie was here
he prophesied
his own eventual absence.
Held the door in his hand.
Pulled closed the whole house
and was gone
knowing the drive here and home
as the final ordeal.

And my aging uncle
cannot rise from the strawberries
once he's there on the earth
kneeling among those red-hearted rows
his hands a heavy crimson
with the blush of harvest
like the miraculous bleeding
of a costermonger's Christ.
But he cannot rise ...
my father laughs beside him
how helpless he's become
though there's sibling sorrow
where a man might rub his thumb
on life
and the moments that make him
less tall than himself
when he's down on his knees
in a field called forever.

And this last visit
my father reminds me
how he can't any longer drive in the dark
how the distance from home
is a circle
he'll measure by lamp harps
to the names of the towns he might touch
till the cruel of the evening
steals daylight
on the wintering away of roads.

Somewhere Inside My Father

Somewhere inside my father
like the silk scarf of the soul
is the boy
who once ate an entire bunch
of bananas
at a single sitting.
They must have hung awhile
like a drooping cluster
of garish yellow unsold over-sized gypsy earrings
almost all the same size
hanging as hunger lamps
in that country pantry
of his youth
where mice made oat marks
like dragged branches
leaving behind the careless attitude
of their appetites
in cupboard gnaw
and the hard-pebbled pellets
of their own refusal to die
anywhere else but there
with the red blood beads
of their last trap-breathing
so beautiful hideous
a little girl might make
a necklace from mortality
and wear it
all day Sunday until bed …

But there in the bone palace
of my father's full-man self
also like a wheat hull
blowing about a barn floor
is the thought
of the boy who poked the mud below the pond
moving toward his older sister
who on the hill
in dresses blew away
like smoke from blazing branches
which dims the colour of all that it caresses
while dogs of the distant past
lie sneezing in the burning dark.

Most Nights Weeping

the dear old man
says he falls asleep
most nights weeping
for his three lost sisters
and I wonder
what's the clever
anti-sentimental point
of bookish and cynical intelligence.

Egyptians
mummified the dead
removing the brain   first
drawing it out through the nostrils
like broken-nose wadding
because they thought it
entirely unimportant
the ancient Chinese believed
the heart
was the seat of thought
imagine, Nietzsche's bleak cardiogram
his heart
black as a bachelor's roast
the cat
who ate Thomas Hardy's heart
the grief
that rescued Shelley's
heart from flames
like a red bouquet of unrejectable roses
the sixteenth century
medical miracle

of the man with the window
in his ribs
he could open
like a door of a cage
on a palpitating crimson

the plush satin interiors of an expensive clock
I hear in these
the litany of lovely rhythms
dead languages – Latin
and its final ulularum
the Greek thesaurus
the Greek kukula
the Mayan Chichen Itza and
Tulum
the way blood
arrives in seas of darkness
like a floating demijohn
of Homer's most empathetic word for wine

The Man with One Hundred Watches

Oh wind my heart
like a bachelor's apple
and give my father half
he loves his watches so!
Old ontological gods amaze themselves
to think of him
and jewelers beggar their shops
though they alchemize immortality
and measure time
to the very tick of doom
what's a singularity to Dad
and what's a string of booms
he's such a heavy coat
a laden arm
a bedroom's busy bureau drawer
and when a little girl
or boy
might have turned an empire to and fro
to find the name that loves them
or spun a snow stem till it snapped
on 'c' or 'd' or over-wound a northern spy
like someone setting back the sun
the windowsill
had held awhile to ripen peaches by ...
I'll take his silver sleeves
his buckled pulse
his dozen faces and his score of hands
the little inner springs as strong as spider silk
the throbbing summer jewels away
the hundred-sectioned autumns
cidering brown the ground and
weathering into lengthening sleeps
of sheep counts
into morning

and then they count themselves

The Art of Shaking Hands

my father is teaching my sons
the protocol for the art of shaking hands
as then he offers his arm
"Dewey Affleck shook hands like this," he says
and he's weak as a waterless weed
as limp as the sleeve of a coat on a man half-dressed
as if he were only recently dead
or feckless from a fever
or he'd suffered a wound in the war
on that side

as for me
I learned from the best
I've made men wince
and drop to their knees
I've sent women weeping
and walking away
I've been lashed by the tongues
of the injured
gripping their rings
"I've arthritis," they say
"have a care."

and what have my boys felt
as they stand
by the willowy droop
of the lesson they're laughing to learn

I think of the grief
I have caused
with my grip
as if holding a child near a well

"hello," I might say
"you won't drown …"

not as long as my father's alive
in this fist.

Bright Red Apples of the Dead

there is courage in plums
and pears
locked as they are
in the high yellow youthful
appetites of the summer sun
what with
the mutable knowledge of falling
so shamelessly smooth
they seem
in their seams and creases
in their rounds
and clusters to affect
the same impudicity as impubes
climbing naked among leaf shake
and stem rattle
where breath plays out the light
like failure of lamp haloes
in the metal harps
and burnt papers
of old houses
where men might smoke and read
or women rush
their wools to the final farmer's pearl

*

And my father's last words before dying
"I want one red apple"
occur as caution
to the orchard
and the never-lasting heart shape
of a deep red shelter
pip to pulp
oh, what a sleeve-shined candy
what a sweet enliven
in the broken flavour of language
what's a watch-wind
to the windfall
in the palming off of autumn
what a sound-soft of dark green knocking
what a shakedown before cider
floating to their bruise-brown
like the gentle settle
of a thoughtful teacup
at the sipping out of story
leading into laughter

*

as with when my father was a schoolboy
who tore the seam out of his trousers
and he stood beside the bell-pull in the long hall
after recess
bending over wagging to the rhythm
as with his scrotum gonging
to make his classmates clatter with mirthful watching
much like a good ram walking

*

and I thought
as I heard
this gentle swing and clangor
"ask not for whom the bell tolls"
and I changed a single vowel
into chortles with the telling
as with the taste of sleeping
as with the scent of blossoms
as with the sight of tree junk burning
as branches fever into darkness
as with the sound
of apples rolling
into bentwood of wet baskets
as with the touch of bright wings brushing
to the lasting loss of colour
and such a pulp-weight of brown remember
like the tanning temples of the sun-changed mind
I am sad
for apples unattended
and I shape a palm-up sorrow
for their wither

Trucker Angels

I was washing my hands
in a roadside room
two men I hardly noticed
were standing beside me
their conversation
a blur beneath water plash
and warm palm blow
and also the come and go of others
among whom I was one
of the many
where time broke its strand
and spun out a little slower
thinned to a lengthening blue
like sparrow thread
about to become songless bricolage
under wing weight
and the empty promise of beauty
brushed to shape and shine
but I was
there locked and lost
in the secret silence of myself
grieving the rush
of my father's shade
three days faded
into the aching all-about
recurrence of brilliance and dark
and as I laved my lifeline
to the pulse point
I heard two words emerging
as it is with buoyancy
or the coming clear of stones in fog

"John's father"
lifted from the line
and wove out from the fabric of their language
then
settled into insentience, pulled
either way from there.

In afterthought
I wondered were they angels
come as truckers
sent to fold their wings
as shoulder tension
in their shirts
to tell me something
concerning the passing away of men

as it is with 'said things'
and the slightly soapy fragrance
of remember
I want to return and ask
them "might I have
my father back"
just for a while
just long enough to listen …

Child's Time

in those days of my boyhood
my father would leave me, like a dog
alone in the car, parked
outside the local village meeting place
and he would simply say
"you stay there, I'll be back in a minute"
which meant an hour
in child's time
but I was obedient as stone
so there I sat
like a package
learning the meaning
of still
forgiving even the barber
who blamed me, squirming
for clipping my ear
the canon who glowered down
from the pulpit
like a captain watching the deep for the drowned
my uncle, the vicar, requiring quiet
the library silence of Sunday
the wag of his grandfather clock
like an upside down piano
pendulously counting the shadows of play
with us as noiseless as hunters
our haloes like circles in pools
oh, what we were
stiff as the posture of dolls
we sat with the fold of our hands
on the desks at our school
like the shaping of prayer
in photographer's light

but back to the boy in the car
where I waited like books piled in a stack
to be read
I waited like bales in the sun
like cut thistles drooping in sheaves
perhaps, at the end of my life
I'll want that time back

for now, I'll simply relive
the ease of his exit
the pause on the street of return
"now, that wasn't too long"
he might say
with the scent of each word
in the mind
like the salt of the nut he's consumed

*Thirty-Three-Thousand
Shades of Green*

The Day the Planes Flew In

The day the planes
flew in
like fireballs
twin towers fell to dust
collapsing to a crush
of dream.
And people of an ancient ash
as primitive as chiseled stone
emerged in weirdly silent
gauzy groups ghosted by smudge
as widows in our midst
do sometimes dress themselves in grief.
And there upon the fatal island
all our loss
was gathered by a cindered cloth
that someone shook
to shroud the burning mountain
of our sorrow in.
The clarifying isinglass
of milky air
divides us as an
isotherm might spin its
unseen silk upon a loom of wind
and we are of a single weather
pole to pole.

In Washington
a tiny klatch of chambermaids
is gathered chatting in the street
outside a grand hotel
as empty as a hollowed gourd

and in that sweet-ache circle
the language breaks
upon the tongue
as birds crack seeds
to make a fertile field
beneath a future flight

and what it means
is in the drift of breath
and blow of skirt
and what it means
is in the weep of weeds
and what it means
is in the way we hold the past
unfolding a precious handkerchief
in which we keep
gold rings, dried flowers
wisps of infant hair

grandfather's rusted gun.

Until the Stars that Are Not There Have Disappeared

poem written after the collapse of the Twin Towers of New York City

I am in a lineup
on the stairs
descending
from the stars that are not there.

My face has burned the window
passing as does the frost
as does the ghost of dust
that's left from the millenary faith of moths in light.
Mine are rain shadows
that haunt the lazy glass.
Mine are the gauzy webs
of a wedding
when the bride has married sorrow
to a spider skein
and kept unending vigil
with an attic veil.
My visage swims the sticky nets
drowned sailors find
in deep repose
as fishermen haul forth from fathoms
their weighty death
where mermaids flag their fins
and slip away from grief.

I am in line
upon the stairs
descending
from the stars no longer there.
I shall not step
lest I should fly.
I shall not step
lest I should fall.
I shall not step
until the stars no longer there
have disappeared.

The Photograph is Actually That of David Peel

Everything is everything.   Bruce Springsteen

Gravity is a predicament.
When we die standing
we fall.
The shock of it suddenly goes
deep into the earth
as moles seeking to solve
impossible tangles
of subterranean trees might also find
the difficulty of stone
the seep of soak
the slow collapse of sand
with the weight of someone walking
the smallering darkness.
And if by dogs
if by foxes
the star-nosed mole of the soul
should go below farm-well fathoms
to push lost labyrinths
beyond a wet line
he'll flood himself floating
as it is with storm sewer and river swell
and the dry rain of rising tide.

And we find that home
is amazing peril ...
the soap is waiting underfoot and foolish
the radio frays its chord
blue fire belches and blooms
the foxglove releases its garden digitalis
into the bitter tea of an aching heart
the apple pip breaks white
and thins the blood

we do the dead man's float
for hours
stumbling in the beautiful suburban pools
our blond hair floating a lightless halo
as we sink
reflected apples
with the weight of nothing
bob above us where the mind belongs.

America the Beautiful

"I looked in the bag and saw a bullet proof vest and the bottom of the bag was covered in fuckin' bullets!"
        cell phone conversation overheard on the way to the World Trade Centre
        June 8, 2016

she was loud, nonplused
careless of being overheard
as she walked away
from the *Path*
on her way into the ruins
of Jersey City
she came up out of the underground
like Persephone
moving through black smoke
among wild stone horses
the froth of their manes
smouldering
over her naked shoulders
like cold steam

and she entered
the myth of America
as though the dark conflagration
of innocent death
were as purposeful as yawning at violence
and the ethereal ennui of gunfire
in the streets of south Chicago
gunfire at Sandy Hook elementary school
gunfire in a gay club in Orlando

remember the efflorescent rifle muzzles
of the sixties, daisy stems
pushed into weapons of the national guard
like the rubber-tipped
spring-loaded toy darts of childhood, something
awful is going *pop pop pop*
in the neighbourhoods of night, and

I am brought by this
to consider
the three thousand names on the walls
of ground zero
the weird metallic Oculus
blooming as a bruised and gargantuan sculpture
built out of broken steel
from the brought-down buildings of Lower Manhattan

and I ask a woman
working every day
in the white-winged shadow
of that sharp-edged colossus
"What is that?"
and though she toils in its shade
has done for the entire two years
of its construction—she says
"I have no idea."

and I think
how *incuriosity* might be
the blandest of all evils –
she's taken her place
among the blameless ignorant
as though
she were already dead
and she simply didn't know or care
or even care to know

A Dark Little Psalm Against War

*poem written after seeing a documentary
on the rise and fall of Adolf Hitler*

lost between fear and the fairgrounds
to the cult of fire
and the idolatry of death
these skull-browed men in red and black
bow to accept bouquets
from barelegged little flower girls
blowing almost away in thin summer dresses
or pat the forehead fidelity of dogs
their own one Führer in final repose
his uniform coat
his pair of pajamas
a burned body in a bomb crater in April
in Berlin bearing the tight-boned grin
of eternity
with sixty-million souls
for company, remembering
those sentimental interludes
that poisonously sweet teacake ambrosia
tasting of the smoke of burning flesh
and the ash-drift of confection
like a Christmas evening snowfall

oh, the wrong gods are in the mountains
above the overcast
or riding a red river of crushed roses

when weeping and harp-willowed
is the world
it dashes our children on stones.

Taking the Pulse of the Tortured Man

"my former interrogator held my hand ... gripped my wrist and told me that when I was being tortured, he measured my pulse ..."
Eric Lomas from The Railway Man

the small Japanese officer
Nagase Takashi, when he tortured
the railway man at Kanchanaburi bridge
during the heat of bridges in a terrible war
he took and gentled his English arm
as a father might
that of his sleeping daughter
set dreaming on a counterpane
and so – he sought
the pulse points
like the smallest breath
from the quiet prayer of seven faiths
like the blue-grey smudging out
of three brief Buddhist fires
seeking there the weight
that falls from weeping
when the heart within is weak
on the bones of the breast
like grief stroking an oak with a broken rose

and then in the lengthening line of forgiveness in time
the elder oriental seeks his peace
by turning those larger hands
to feel the life
like the dying of rain after rain
as it is with watching the jump of a water-touched leaf
this being the thirst of sorrow
this being the fly at the door

Thirty-Three-Thousand Shades of Green

an artist friend said this morning
there are thirty-three-thousand
shades of green —
and afterwards I watch
the television image
of the drone of a midnight mosque
in war
which seems
the sunken tower of a ship
lost beneath the aqua filters of a distant sea
this doomed green city of Iraq
drowned in deep-water dark
so weirdly avocado-coloured
in this visionary light
where cars come eeling out along the street
to slip the shaded bottle bubbles
like a loss of breath
in burning saints and dying sailors
saying last farewells from spirit fathoms of their over-heavy selves

and birds in flight
come swimming on like sudden moths
white-mossed and myrtle
to the moon
as small gay brooches
of a running girl's delight
they flitter off these branches
and are gone
to milt the tarnished edges of our sight
oh what a verdant
batholith is builded there
beneath some ancient heaven's unpresumptive blue

but now that hour sleeps
beyond a shipwrecked sun
as thirty-three-thousand greens
float up like shoe-stepped grass
to catch
the after-sap of also-greening stars.

Watching the Italians

Sometimes I will sit for hours
watching foreign-language television
listening to Cantonese views
imagining comprehension
of oriental concerns
with all those brilliant silks
and the pyrotechnics of joyful
draconology in the wiser streets
of ever-bustling duck-proud Chinatown.
I love the sweet
and often-overlong ghazals
sung to the singsong suitcase wheeze of the shruti box
by bird-bright voices of Punjab.
O tonic drone
my soul responds
like light through troubled smoke.
The Spanish talk shows
entertain me with their rolling rs
and high-toned women
with raven hair so unashamed
of beauty that their mouths
become the bloody red of budding summer roses.

And also
the genius of German
is lovely to my ear
Ich lebe mein Leben in wachsenden Ringen
die sich über die Dinge ziehn.
ah Rilke
I too *live my life in growing orbits*
which move out over the things of the world.

And this morning
bored and angry from
the empty endlessness of CNN
and their mostly vacuous coverage
of yet another WAR
I change the channel
and find myself
watching the Italians
whose camera suffers to show
the wounded and the weeping
the bandaged girls and broken boys
the recently widowed men embracing father sorrow
beyond the smudge of rubble houses
collapsed in rising dust and burning stone.

Meanwhile outside my home today
the sky above my winter garden shines an incandescent blue
a single cardinal
lands upon my frosted fence, his shadow
black against the phosphorescence
of the snow.
He burns to the very flicker
of his sheltering wings
with such a red
he's like the sacred hearts
of Catholic devotion
in the paintings of Freda Kahlo

and I am here
locked in this almost silent western choir
looking to where one dove
sits grooming on a post.
Both he and post are driftwood grey
I swear it's true
and when I look up again from this most fatal page

he's gone
like sadness softened over time
but we are in the midst of terror
trivialized
and loss of life
is one immortal absence
well beyond the dark-green glamour
of a turned-off TV screen.

His Change of Heart When it Comes to War

my mother calls me naïve
and says
in the war
meaning her war
meaning World War II
with all the news of home
in the sad slow unfolding of things
when things have yet to occur
where she wept
for her favourite cousin
shot playing possum
trembling among the truly dead
and the heart went out of him
so when he arrived
at the Woffenden's his last summer
while his two legs slept all day
and would neither wake nor walk his weight
their whole length pruned of purpose
in that soul-dark hour
when broken life falls on its own shade
no longer owned and *who am I*
to contradict such truth
and grieving
who am I to question
the old ancestor time
with fractured hip and lacerated hand
who took a musket ball
and lived on half-ruined
with sword-sheath palms
almost a hundred years after
who am I to knife his heart
and call him wrong
among the screaming horses

of his most heroic days
for if I say a jubilant liberation came too late
with forty million ghosts
joining smoke in one beautiful blue and silent heaven
with Hiroshima thinking light
and then a brilliant darkness
who am I to ask the ashes
how many griefs before we learn
how many violent quiets
must we visit here
how many blindnesses
to look upon
encoded in a whispering dust
like the tiny yellow whirlwinds
that follow the farmer walking a well-worked field
with him never looking back, not once

The Covenant

"I do set my bow in the cloud,
and it shall be for a token of covenant between me and earth."
                                                    Genesis 9:13

two men stand
on a seawall
looking east from where Halifax mist
has fractured light
with the web bow bountifully double-arced
under multi-coloured heaven
flung full like two wind-caught bolts of five-hued silk
gone still

not since Noah
not since the waters assuaged
and the rain restrained
and the restless dove returned
not since the ravening dark
long after the antediluvian days
of Adam's third son, the mostly forgotten Seth
with the earth
unpacking her oceans
and all Atlantis drowned
to soul-sweep's sweetening blue
and smouldering gold

on August evening
two friends
took their ease
and watched

while water-broken sky
loomed as lovely luminescence
over the wharf
in frames that could not hold
the slip away
of moments into memory.

But Where Were the Horses Of Evening

On a nearly perfect summer evening of my third sojourn at the Trappist monastery of Gethsemani located in the green and verdant heart of rural Kentucky, fellow poet, Roger Bell and I sat taking our ease at the edge of bean field in the shadow of a residence the monks refer to as "the studio". We were talking in low and reverential tones, our voices almost subsumed by the loud insect choir of stridulating katydids and singing crickets, the cicadas' hour already having passed. Roger was waxing nostalgic about the long lost bluebirds of his Port Elgin childhood. I was lamenting a life bereft, for I had never seen a bluebird, though I'd heard rumours of their sometime presence in my own home county. Just as we spoke of these blue-feathered, red-breasted beauties, one lit on the ground before us as if our longing had called it out of the gloaming.

In the morning, with the post-dawn mist still clinging to the pond, Roger drew me from my slumber to see where the horses were standing at the gate to the pasture.

In the company of poets, I have gone on annual journeys to Abbey of Gethsemani for the past five years. I have made good friends. I have spent time in meditation contemplating my faith. While there, I have been visited in dreams by demons and angels. The poems in *But Where Were the Horses of Evening* arise from the synchronicity of sacred ground. These poems are for my companions and fellow retreatants, Marty Gervais, Roger Bell, Hugh MacDonald, Paul Vasey, Marilyn Gear Pilling, Mary Ann Mulhern, and for my Kentucky pal, Bob Hill and most especially for Brother Paul Quenon whose spiritual mischief delights us all.

But Where Were the Horses
 of Evening

The horses are eating the fogs of the dawn
it has whitened their bones
like birches, their hearts become
stone under foam
they drum to the withers
in rivers of burning
they come to the fences
a-smoulder and vanish
like blown-away breath
in the vapour of naming
their manes
like what clings
to the sashes worn ragged
at the fringes of windows
of houses
they stand
in wet grasses
brown-girthed to grey vapour
as if they were floating
great boats of bent ribs
arriving or leaving
adrift on far meadows
grown calm after heaving
and slowing their breathing ...

last night
was loneliness lovely outside
by the bean field
the fireflies flickered
like stars we were dreaming
friend Roger in doorlight
while old heaven showed
in the wet of the pond
how it was
aging with faith in the failures
of moonlight forgetful
in cloud-cross like losses
from memory sleeping
but where were the horses
of morning–I wonder
where were they waiting
what elsewhere was in them
what linger of distant green hunger
the grasses were building
from darkness
to bless us in daylight
to fill our sad bodies
like vases of silence
with silence

Why am I the One taken for a Monk Among five friends on a Bench in front of Thomas Merton's Hermitage

There are five of us, seated
as on a bench facing the camera
and I am the fifth
the one on the right
the tallest, the only one wearing
sunglasses, the only one
with legs ankle-crossed, and though
my wedding band seems obvious
when strangers to us all
play 'guess-the-monk' they guess at me

"he's the monk" they say
pointing at the man I know the best

and what I remember of the day
we spent walking
the wet green, pausing to consider
the long grasses in bloom, to debate
by book and leaf-saw variety
the wild indigenous vegetation
of the mind-seen meadow
isn't there in the photograph
where we pose in a line like gas-station reg'lars

perhaps, I am the only one
who looks truly beatific
the only one who looks like someone
not about to say something
to the absent photographer
to the lonesome camera resting on a rail

　　　　　Roger's head says, "thermometer"
Marty's is framed by shutters
Hugh's Yankee hat flies between window wings
and he's become an insect iridescent
Brother Paul shimmers glass-blue above the skull
meanwhile my thought balloon
is pre-filled by the word 'shalom'
fixed and posted by the door
the only thing I could possibly be thinking
provided by that cinder-block blessing
which would if it could   but it can't   float away...

Walking with Brother Paul

for Marty

morning at Gethsemani
an early fog
seems like lime dust lifting thickly to the light
as the monastery spire
withers at the height of new heat
like altar snuff
and we enter the sounding forest
walking the wide path
bruising green with heavy bent-weed dew
while the yellow engine of the day
is rounded almost white
as milk that's not quite cheese
set in the clabber gauze of thinning cloud

but everything burns
as it is with wet hiss
of stone in ash and old fire
smouldering
at the torpid locus of steam
and the land groans large
as it goes suddenly grey-dry
like book dust and miller wing
and wheat hull
and dead locust found in grain
that might smudge
the thumbs of sad starved farmers
yet here
cicadas sing in mad chorusing choirs
of slow saws
whining in tough cuts

building their bent circles
from before and after the loud ages
of ugly insect hallelujahs
that surround us and round us out
and measure where we are in time
from the first hour
of our going to the last

into this thousand-acre furnace
until down in the tortoise cloister
of a gully

we come sweating in self-swelter
breathing like rope length dragged by bell gong

and we arrive, two of the three of us
swooning like soup spoons
save Brother Paul
who is lean and cool in white
within the wide
shadow of his oversized straw fedora

two hours we walk
pausing only twice
once at a well
where we soak and slake
and rest
at the wheeze and prime
of a loose-handled pump
that gushes and chokes
and catches its breath in the bellows
like a weeping child

and when we are done
we stand heavy-wet in our clothes like peeled peaches
as if we'd walked to the throat
through a swale
so when we are naked-damp
in the cool humour of the common showers
we take an oath against walking
with Paul

like boulders in storm
like colossal statues of an ancient world
like the heavy heads of dying husbands
like people protesting the bomb
people blocking bridges
of doomed cities
like skulls on gates
like the limestone-bearded gods of waterfalls
like hundred-year old rain-carved oak
or the salt
that glances at burning

we will not move again
come find us, we are sage as mountain faces
we are Buddha-wise
we are become
the meaning of *metaphysical*
ask us again and again what you will
we will answer only as echo
from within a stillness
that is not sloth
but learning.

Alone

a Gethsemani retreat

How *in the night* I am
clothed in the close torpor
of Kentucky heat
in this monastic room's retreat
of cinder block
and troweled stone
feeling also the false wind
of an oscillating fan
rotating its blow-page blur
like an owl on a post
too wise to wink
watching for a path of prayer

and in this fan force
from this desk
through this open wall
I see
the glowworms
flash and fade
like sparks expiring
from the spirit blaze
of Merton's famously burning barn
as fickle-tindered and mostly out of fuel
where forest greets the shade
that shadows
into something large—too large
and far too far

moving toward the past
beyond the fatal grief of close-by graves
that grieve no more
but mossed to an indifference
lean on sleep
within the moody moisture
of that slow horizon's
lost constellations
reconfigured by an insect sky
dropped down to find their heaven on the earth
become a mostly discontinuous light

and meanwhile later
in the ever-spiritual centre of the dark
I'm visited by a demon in a dream
which like a sheet that slips the bed
is but a spectral drift
frail eidolons of drowning fear
in water shifts
and shell shoals
broken by a gentle wash
and shallow tide
moon veils my body barely feels

and that same incubus
returns the second night
as from a God-bricked slumber
I wake and wake and wake and wake again
to look upon the clock
that marks my dumb regard
at 1:23, 2:23, 3:23, 4:23, 5:23
the crimson numbers
sere as cattle brands of iron glow

and when I see
the insect-darkened yard
I watch what falls away
beneath the monastery gate
where these two chiseled words
–God Alone–
appear
and though I've entered here
the coffee drinker of the soul's insomniac
arriving where
grey hills adjustment to the fog seems much
like sugar sunk in tea
yet I am drawn
to that out-there
as sharp cicadas saw
the cypress
with dull-toothed sound
and old aromas
lift against what comes with rain.

Washing the Cheese

Brother Paul is washing the cheese
in the cool basement of the monastery barn

otherwise in the small hours
it would surely come shawling
in living veils of mould
like the ghosts of brides
who've married the darkness

and when they wed
these children of christening curd
these lovely confirmations of milk
must be bathed each morning by monks

to have learned
what it means to life to be life left in shadow

like mist on a monument
fog on the cross on the hill
webs of dew on the stone of old graves
a smoulder of beauty left all night burning.

Monks in the Mammoth Caves

deep within the place of peace
in the central chamber
of Mammoth caves of Kentucky
the Dalai Lama came
with his holy message
where the drone of Tibet
joined the Trappist
glory of western voices in song and prayer
and that is also where
they mined saltpeter to form
the powerful powder
that would feed three American wars
from the first revolution
to the smaller flint and pan of a second aggression
to the fiercer guns of the great and terrible
conflagration between brothers
while there like trolls
cruel hands came scrabbling
the walls
like long incarcerations
there in monastic music
they fought the three fires of the world

greed, anger and foolishness   singing

replace the flame of greed with the flame of a generous heart
replace the flame of anger with the flame of a gentle mind
replace the flame of foolishness with the flame of a wise soul

light the way to the world with burning hands
that flash like the wings of brilliant birds
keeping a balance
on lines of fire

Where Silence is The Light

I owe the earth such gratitude
for this briefly borrowed dust
from ancient wonder breathing
to each new delight
the fragrant lingering
aromas of an eternal sea
have thimble wells in us
half-lit pink light
for the thumbnails of the salty heart
those blood moons
to draw three waters
of my inner life.

I skate upon that one desire
that thrills me solid
as a self-born child
meanwhile dog-joy tumbles through the thin design
and leaps out wet
and lapping snow
toward the cheer-chilled house
and I am river's heaven then
upon that frozen floor
steel-thirsty flashing lines
and hollow cut-sounds
of a season's underflow.
And I am also
fog-fond as a valley horse
half-sculpted on a hill
that whetstone
God lifts and turns
to the withers fathom of what's beyond the looking light
those ghost legs sunk into a formless plinth

that holds the standing girth
like breathing barrels
trussed for carrying the beast
occurring only
as a portion of itself.

My soul thirst
ancient and my true thirst new
I'm at the last mirage
arriving everywhere at once
I drink illusionary
permanence and smile
to sift away
into the saying dark
where silence is the light
the poem shadows from.

Simply to Be Seen

I was sitting indoors
watching fog drift
in gauzy teasels
against glass
like the briefly eternal ghosts
of abandoned houses
dragging thought against memory
with the lovely ephemerally lonely mist
of illumination almost there
in the real crest and fall
and sheer of tattered vapour smouldering away
from the cool grey burn of the lost green monastery lawn
and I was listening to Paul talk
about another long ago day of rain
he said
"the best ball game I ever saw
never happened"
as he weathered this sunless hour
with the lyrical bat-crack of his voice
striking true to the stitch
and arc of story whitened by remembering
what it means
to have what we thought we'd wanted
withheld and replaced
by a better longing
—the one we did not know we felt...

Later someone struck a match
to bonfire junk and tree loss and lit outdoor tinder
in a red leap and grey crush
of differently connected things
what heaven received
and what earth required
was in us always, in the bone cathedral
of branches burning
simply to be seen.

Loosening Green–An Excursion at the Monastery

We long
to simply *walk away*, out
beyond the circle of embrace
outside the echolalia of flesh
and the pulming of the close-hearted
where the fierce concern
of human love
has lost its pull and push
where we are loosened green, strolling lonely
in the rise and fall of land
where the only language
is the language of birdsong
and the loud Eros of insects
calling and crying in wild striding
stridulation and chirrups of heat
like moisture singing from branches in flame
where even the least
and smallest movement of weather
comes ghosting its breath in tall corn
exhaled through the shaken-silk summer of fields
and you were there
to lead me to those old
striations of lime
this ancient cliff face
rising through scre and slopes of lost soil
to be set like the geological weight
of another age
this stone to clock the seasons
where faces emerge
from shale erosions
to ancestor dawn among these
scrub pine broken by rain

yet on this day they were hiding
in light loss from you
though I saw the old man of the stone
I showed him
shouldered and framed by the thrust
of an alder
his one eye feathered
in fern, yet
you did not see him at first
for you he'd sunk into grey, into this hour of shade
amorphous and formless as plaster-to-walls
"it must be the light"
you were saying
and we wondered what fears us
in curious ways
or longs to reveal the wells of itself
to one soul at a time
when then, just then, a ragged winged
tatter of daylight alive
landed from trouser and leapt
to the back of my hand
to drink at the web in its delicate way
like a thread that was mending a veil.

Something So Ugly

I've plucked a fractured portion
of box turtle shell
from the monastery mud
"May I keep it, Brother?" I ask...
"Why would you want
something so ugly?" Paul says—But look
what I lift from the muck
like a rind from a gourd
though broken and peeled holds beauty
torn from the spine of a life
like a potter's lost shard.
It cracks from a dip in the clay.
It leaks rain
at the tail
and has left a five-vertebrae back
in the dish
like the bones of a meal from the hungers of time.
Its interior's tainted with moss
and the lines on the dome in decline
like old paint on the frame of a door
and it's dusted
with dirt from the tortoising earth
such a terrapin absence
is here
such reptilian emptiness
it's flaking of colour
like chitin from beetle back shuck
translucent in light
and ancient as mouths.
I am painting the universe brown
there's an honour in tan
among stars I have seen
where space is bland as an egg.

with no individual darkness
but this
that fossils us
close to old stones
the amphibian faith in a choir is futuring
night with deep noise, the heat
of cicadas in song
tomorrows the edges of dusk
and the sheddings
of heaven are also at home
as linens inhabit a trunk
without locks
when the bride is a century cold.

God Bless

God bless these holy bones
my body's but a guesthouse
for the soul
although the sea has its perfumes
a season in the flesh
this prayer of kisses
often salty crowned
these words
the mud-shaped movement
of breath-watered clay
I'm God's enoughness
for a while
loosening the knots of time
to be the wind
within an empty palm
or blow the hands away
like sand
I touch my brow
with thanks
and tip my fingers
to a far farewell
that redolence caressed like night by fragrant dreams
my life's
an absent ocean ever-present
in a vacant shell

The Colder Light
for Marty Gervais

My God
doesn't even believe
in himself
I say and I see
him write it down
and call it wise

well as for me
I'm looking for love
in the worm-lost word
for the way we kiss

how time
consumes time
in the folded hold
of a hole in space
and I meet myself
in the star-black burn
of miraculous touch

what am I then
but reflected smoke
from that second fire
the colder light
of watershine that cannot be itself

Walking Past Cow-Barn Lake
for Brother Paul Quenon and Mary Ann Mulhern

This is the way
we carry the names

the cows
are the light on wild grass
the barn
is unbuilt by the clock
in the weeds

but the water remains
where the fence
is a ghost
of sprung wire
and the posts
are letting it go
in the lean of old dowel
where the earth
is a saw of wet rot

but the pond
is still holding the sky
and my face
is cloud-fraught and clear
but I am not
there when I'm here

though I carry
my name
like the wind.

I Might Say

There are things I might say
were I here.

I believe in God
because He's the best story
I know.

I'm sick of
the science of time.

I'm sick from American news.

If that is the truth,
I refuse.

I'm important, you see.
I'm a dog in the sky.

It's my universe
and I claim it as mine

and I'm leaving my scent on the stars.

Living at the Monk Motel

I wake in the morning
to the crimson hallelujah
of divine sunrise
burning off the last vestiges
of vaporous darkness
with the slow coming on
of consciousness after dreaming
only the visible spire
and the white stone architecture
of the Abbey's clarified geometrics
breaking through the pines
with its bells calling out for the earth's
deep attention
gonging through the groomed hills of Gethsemani
over the grave thoughts of the dead
in the yard as ghostly companions
to the meditative garden
only these human interruptions
corrupting the wild
insalient and always worshipful
choirs of cold-light cicadas
sawing their wings into wilderness choirs, this
and the insuppressible urgency of birdsong
celebrates daylight and silence

and that we are humans then
comes true in the body
as bones, locked
in otherwise golden inches
where pleasure
pours dark honey of heart blush
to the pulse points of temple and wrist, my words
like cut grass falling
at the meaningful edge of the meadow
with its redolent fragrance of clover's
interweaving perfume
unseen in tall timothy
grown wishful of seeding

What Burns Through Remember

at the side of the path
through the forest
on Gethsemani grounds
the poisonous vines
rise in the bark of the oak
on woody stems
like the veins on a weightlifter's arms
they are serious sermons
about reaching the sky
they are lifting
green leaves to the light
with their venomous oils
snaking through shade
their tri-leaf toxins
warning the darkness
I've come
with a shadow of blood
to bully the beat of the heart
with an old osmosis
I'm binding red welts
to the flesh
like the lash of a whip
I'm licking
the earth like a wound
in the clay
with blisters of rain

as for me
when I was a child
I saw
with such fear
as one feels as a youth
God's love
for the sparrow in song
or his love for the rat
in the grain
the strong brute rubbed a girl's face
washed her in weed
so she swelled
as though she were falling asleep
in the crimson scald of his rage ...

and that was the way
what burns
through remember
like vapor through smoke
with a match in the mind
called Lucifer
and the sulfurous scent of its light

Let Light Try All the Doors

Echo's Revenge

i

Sit very still
and walk within your body
like a house of many rooms
let light try all the doors
and craft a slowness
where you dream the walls away
and sweep the corners
with a thin white cane
imagine then with such a seeing blindness
all an unseen inner world you hold
against the tip of memory

ii

last week
I was in France
this week, in Seoul
I've lived
the peripatetic summer
of a flibbertigibbet dragonfly
above a water flash
my life become
the shadow flutter
of a mortal thing
going "briefly briefly"
as I beat the ragged membrane of my wet wings

*

there is a gallery I've seen in Seoul
within that current city
at a recent hour
wherein a sculptor sharing my name
has hung a pool of ice-blue cloth
come waterfalling
from a broken branch
it gathered gravity
then flung a spill across a patch of floor
like silence
in a photographic stream
it honoured
lingering and limned
with coolness lovely folds

and rucks of shadowed space
too pale to contemplate
it held itself inhaled
like childbreath to a candlewish

one twig
was swaddled with
a multi-coloured string
like candy swirls
on sweet sticks at a fair

what shadows there were
were but
the uninvolving shades
that catch
the artifice of indoor light
the lux
that's cast from bulbs
like the stains
old paintings leave
upon a paper wall

and what is meaning then
to fix a story
on a patch of sky

we looked and thought
how human
it is to ask

look to the weathered stone
the ancient tree
the place the river
pushes at the sand
the cloud-crossed sun
the gauzy monument
coalescent on a cooling green
the whisper of a flower wind
the flame lean
of a luminescent petal
and the temple of a purple loss
much like
the grief that presses tears

and we consider then
what this might mean
when put to purpose
by the mischief of a cat

how curtains come to claws
and little Echo
left alone
to climb the weave
let slip
like seeking silk of sky

the myth
of unrequited calls

unanswered by the attitude
of loosened stays

undress the heights
and run the weave away

iii

A day before
I stood upon the lookout
at the DMZ
to look at where
old sorrows grieved
the graven hills that greened the north

and saw
a single helmet rusted
with a fatal hole
I thought of Hamlet
and his pretty skull of fools
that lad's "alas"
and all the hollow laughter
of the stars

I also thought
of garden pots
abandoned for their broken clays
that could not hold
their purpose
nor serve the well's worth
of their maker's work
and this was where
the soldier
lost his name
the quiet blushes
him to voiceless hurt

the soul's wind
and the bones of war

what's blood but iron
to the earth

red soil
that someone sorrows for

what might I feel
to run my finger
on a rag of tin

or build back a broken nation
death by death

go home
and carry such an emptiness

to shore against
the fullness of regret

iv

and I have strolled
three markets
in a pair of busy weeks

I've walked
the throngy labyrinths
of sellers' stalls
and tourist shops
in Seoul and Burgundy, Leon
and home

and I am mostly
drawn to coins and stones
and tattered books
I cannot comprehend
who spent, who carved
who wrote, who read
who bent the pages
and what inked what minds
in languages I cannot hear and do not speak

my heart is but an apple
in a glazier's bowl
it settles slowly
on a bruise
and aromatizes the glass
that none may touch but I

and thus there is a threshold in myself
I cannot cross
but once and once alone

I see within the morbid soldier's
dusted health
a disappearance to behold
the helmet
vanished grain by grain

I see the palm
that held the coin
or turned the page
the hand
that hew the chisel
chipped the stone

and hear
the Buddhist temple
with an ancient bell
the knowledge
we surround with gongs
and sacred prayers

the hopeful destination
and the train of dreams
the sojourn and the journey
the heart in constant movement
and the mind at rest

the gift of time
though thoughtful
is also like a thief

v

there is also in the gallery
a sculpture
with a painting swirling
on the cut face of an open branch
flowing out to follow the tree rings where they
shape the seasons under paint
the outer circumference
is old
and cast in fractures
fissuring the surface
with natural nicks and notches
of its fatal hours alive
and at the centre
where the heartwood hardens
in the tight-packed core
there beats a pulse of colours
like the clock of pulses
drawing blueness from the cuff
and to a larger drum

what autumns it has known
are fastened there

four fires
and a burning white

the purity that burdens us
at birth
comes wintering
to a brilliance in what's real.

Handsome in Hanboks

the elderly seamstress
throwing her short arms wide
embraces my wife
about her bosoms from behind
taking her measurements
for the pink silk wedding garment
she is making for the marriage of our son
and his beautiful bride-to-be
and she is laughing like busy shop bells
at the ample endowment of western women
for she herself is small breasted
as a girl
and as for me
she must leap up
like a child after apples
she lifts, arches her feet
stands on tiptoes
tucked in close, but then resorting
to *rock-of-eye* for my broad shoulders
she rolls out a beautiful bolt
of shining blue embroidered fabric
and says in Korean
'there may not be enough in all the orient'
as it flows across the floor
like the lovely return of a slow river

and my son wears a tall hat
and hanbok
and we are swaddled
like broken-rib dancers
my fat sleeves blooming like dream wings
my body caressed
in a weird chrysalis of foreign design
my son's bride comes in with her rose-bow mouth
the confetti-blush of her cheek
her hair held by a long pin
and we must gather up maps
to be near them
we must think across oceans
our voices as thin as the old
we must weave in far winds like the rains
and what is our love into darkness
but the ship of our hearts calmed by sleep.

What I Think

I think today of my son
married in Korea
wearing his hanbok and moja
the black felt hat
of the groom
that made him taller than Lincoln
as he carried his bride
trotting in small circles
in front of the painted landscape
a backdrop of hills and valleys
like it once was for them as children
racing on lawns in summer
and I think of the montera—the matador's hat
and the bull *Poeta* I saw killed
in the cheap brass blare of sunlight in Mexico
I think of the busby and the beefeaters of my honeymoon
in jolly old England
of the deerstalker worn by Ole Hansen
of the raccoon cap of my youth
the shako of British grenadiers, the fedoras come fluttering
down
to the ice in the fifties
like a weird returning of winter waterfowl
I think of the baseball stands in the films of the forties
the uniforms and costumes and attires
of other times and other places
in the history of lives

how the beaver hats of Holland came floating on the river
so the sad village fathers first came to know
the fate of their sons in battle
how old bald heads might rise through water
like stones in streams gone dry

I'd seen ten farmers wearing corn-seed caps
in a restaurant outside Batoche
and gave up the battle for decorum

when I was a boy I wore my own ten-gallon
and saddled the apple graft
and rode orchard shadows
drifting away among leaves like a sugar foot
or I rode the banister
gripping the newel imagining a saddle horn
and shooting my spit-wet pistol

what a little soldier I became
that Christmas my parents bought me
the plastic helmet
what a porkpie *cool*
what a toque
what a wet-wool balaclava
flavoured by cold
tasting like sucked mittens
and cold closets thinned by moths

if I were only a head
I'd want a philosopher's palm
to be fond of my mind
as child of a peach
I'd want a gardener turning
my skull like a gourd on the ground
I'd want a haberdasher
to measure my madness
like sleep measures dream
I'd want a hat for that
blocked wide and wild for a box
full of curious bone

Sleeping Dictionary

We walk the neon streets of Seoul
lost without language
in the luminous forests
of that far away city
where the only landmarks
we have managed to blaze
are to our own hotel
to which we return
like stepchildren following crumbs

we're locked in a labyrinth
of uncomprehended design
warrenning off in every direction
and the home of our son
in the school district of An Yang
near the stoplight at the confluence of busy streets
with the groceteria on the corner
with its aromas of lettuce and thyme

we pace a single square
of urban wilds
alive with light
we stand in fear of strangeness
we manage
to say *kam sa ham ni da*
as if we were grateful for everything
we say *thank you*
like the poor, like the mad
like the sorrowfully addicted
like the war-wounded
like the legless, the abandoned
the orphaned, the hopelessly homeless

the drunk-by-noon loser
the derelict, the exiled
the refugee, like Tarzan
in New York

and we ruffle the pages
of our little sleeping dictionary
like a lousy feathered bird

and we say
the words

which take us rushing by car
to the market
where our son's bride, our new daughter
takes my wife's hand
and leads her like a blindfolded child in a game
of *touch the trinket*
and I taste
the roasted silkworm larvae
with its midnight flavours
like the dark rumour of unborn wings
in the savory chrysalis of peculiar words

and I am home again now, as I write
among these familiars
holding a stone I stole
from the courtyard of the palace

turning it over palm upward in my hand
it is a mortared hermetic
fragment of wall
a paperweight of memory
it holds my life in pages
in a terrifying interior wind

Sex with a Second Woman

we are staying
in a small hotel
in a neon lit An Yang
a hostelry
we have been told
where businessmen
bring their mistresses
as it is openly understood
that any truly urbane marriage
will include
sex with a second woman

and so
one night
my wife and I are riding
the elevator
and a couple
step inside
crowding into the drifting closet
sighing up and down
from floor to floor

the man in the shining Italian suit
looking proud, arrogant
and slightly drunk
occupies his body with the loud silence
of an athlete gone to seed
his companion
shy and blushing
hiding her face behind her hand
seemed as though
she might

vanish if she could
behind the fan of her fingers
because
we all know
the intimate purpose of her presence

I've seen it before
elsewhere
this body language of shame
as it is
with children who are caught
stealing from their mothers
this transformation
of beauty
the pain-filled pettiness
of disappointed desire

the way she dissolves
in the wall
like someone passing
a window
only briefly seen
in the glass
though what remains
wears rouge
smells of oriental orchids
and stale smoke
tries not to breathe
too deeply
closes her eyes, she's
keeping a secret
she is not here
she has never been here
not now, not ever
she is a good girl
the one these two tourists
fail to notice
inside her silk disguise.

Bad Men Come

the young girl walks from the water
transformed like a tree by the sun
she is budding half-naked and blooming
in panties ballooning behind
the cotton translucent like paper in rain
she is watched by her father
who guards her from danger
as she runs among breakers
piping the sand bird boned with true joy
while the long-tail boat that brought them
like goods to the shore
is riding the surf
with the flag of its prow waving red
and this is the edge of Ataman Sea
where time breaks pure glass in the wet
and she is involved in frail wafting of petals like flowers
unlocked in slow shade
hers is an innocent peril
and fierce as the flacking of wings is her father
in this inescapable tide
where Ao Phanag and the islands
are joined by a journey
where the keel cuts white crest like the breast of a bull

and here to this land from American cities
here from Canadian towns
come the cruel and lascivious tourists
who ravage the dreams of young daughters
in rents of the night torn thin
like old silk that fades at a fold

what a scatter of stars is my soul
what a waste of the haloes of heaven
like finding my heart in a bowl
mostly meat for the flies in the market
mostly eaten away like spoiled fruit.

Tuk-tuks in Bangkok

Riding through the busy streets of Bangkok
in a three-wheeled tuk-tuk
we are putt-putting and tilting along
as if we were floating in a little-boy's boat
too fast for the water
the unsure gunnels of our chromium rails
wobbling like oarlocks
rocked by fools
we go the wrong way
wheeling through traffic, weaving and
waving into the hubbub and hurly burly
of horns and headlights
on a path to the golden Buddha
gilding upward like a sunlit fish
later we climb the stone steps
and touch the tiles of an ancient temple
the one of which my aunt might have said
"you've seen one, you've seen
them all ..." and there are
ten thousand in the city
which last evening was littered with late-night sleepers
families dreaming in street cots
under shop awnings

all day we laugh along
wagging like fat-bottomed clowns
and no matter how often I'm told not to
I knock my skull on the surrey fringe
of the tuk-tuk roof getting in getting out
so the driver smiles and winces
with worry
for the poor Canadian tourist
too tall for his brain
with its memory rivers
and recent rains
drenching inward like a watercolour
too wet to hang

the driver says he is a student
who works all day
and studies at night
so he must be done by five
go home and dress in the uniform of scholars
—black pants, white shirt
school tie—he smiles like money
dumps us off at the low wall
 surrounding the palace
says "you're on your own now"
as he leaves us lingering and lost
in the slow fumes of cheap fuel
half-burned gasoline
atomizing the air
like the pulse points of shop girls
working on the broken engines
of the heart

Thai Boxer
for Dylan

the Thai boxer
in the photograph
fanning his arms in the dark
achieves
the blur of wings
and so
violent angel
in the smoke light
of an outdoor bar
becomes
the heavy bird
exhausted
by the bone weight of the sky
he falls as *soul*
into the gravity
of gloves and boots
as colour
runs in water
down a weeping glass
upon a ruined window   painted
after rain

hold up
this simple image
and transform
the chrysalis of man

we cannot see ourselves
but how we're made to see
and we are blind

Ten Days Out of Step with the Sun: a poem on the tsunami

> *by the time of the European Renaissance Caesar's calendar had drifted ten days out of step with the sun*
>
> from *A Short History of Progress,*
> by Ronald Wright

those buoyant swimmers off the shore
felt it first
as but a gentle undulation of the sea
they rose and fell
upon the briefly deepening swell
that rocked
their snorkels like wind-stirred reeds
and gave their breath a sleepy nudge
above the yellow swarms
and weaving heaves of fish electric blue
they moved below the light
to watch the stingray's lashing tail
the essing of the eels
while water birds
cast shadows on the foam
the wet mosaic of each sickled wing, their cries
repeating loneliness and joy

and then the shore refused them
in a single wash
the startled thousands
smothered as they smiled
and one wave amazed the windows
with its liquid voice
to set the earth a vasty nanosecond
out of time
the watch adrift
the calendar wrong
the moon's amazement
at the fatal tide
the season's swidden

but a cultivated drudge
among the cracking palms
that slashed like fire in the hills
what ancient God we see in this
the Lord of plague and famine
ashing at the blue-rimmed paradise
to wreck our pretty myth
with water's war

the little girl upon her knees
beside her frilly bed
can't breathe
what slides between my hands:
the silk of faith
the scarf of strangled dreams

Ghosts in the Mud
Phi Phi Island eight months after the tsunami

the sand-and-butter books lie lost
breathing mud like a drowned gills
half buried among the detritus
of water's retreat
one beautiful pottery shard
that my son plucks
like a petal from the tropic smother
of clothing and bricks
he knows I'll take it home for souvenir
the only lovely thing he sees is shining blue

the boatman tells us
how he lost two customers
as the waves came closing together
from two directions
rising to a crest
like the terrible wing strokes of a warring angel

he points
to where he climbed
the tropic palm close by, climbed it to its tattered fronds
says how the water crafted wreckage
lifting boats on swells
as they vanished like floating soap

and I look
to the ruined roof edge
to the wreck of shingles
torn from the trough line
of a closed up hotel
and I see
in the rubble how ugly it was
to be there

and in the blue glaze
of what's broken to hand size
I'll carry the beauty of ghosts in old ceramic fireclay

as we rest in the shade of our sorrow
where the water is gentle today
as careful as delicate children
who rattle white shells
on a thread

and thus beginneth the lesson

we were laved in beauty
standing to the pulse points of our throats
throbbing in the great wide
time-burdened aquamarine waters
of the Indian ocean
where the heart teaches the soul
with each warm caress
this is the burning line
girding the earth with wave upon wave
of salt-swelled matrilineal love
and my son and I were tossing weeds
when I ducked
and one feathered thing flew over my submersion
and struck his mother, my wife
with all the verdant indignation
of a green slap
thus striking from her face
her glasses so they fell
and drowned in a blue-green blur
at her feet
as the world became
a water-washed smudge
of sand-blind glass

and then as if to prove
us all mere dots that bob about in tides
like the bridegroom washed from the rocks
at Peggy's cove
or the man come too close
the lashing surf
lost to the rising
shores
and last seen sinking
in the far-off oceans
where ice floats and slams
white shivers on vanishing surface of light

a semi-translucent lace of jellyfish flesh
drew itself like a knife cut
on her arm
where it welted a blush
in a red-hot splash of pain
like the blood-flame of fever rash
and she thought she might be dying

and yes it could come
that quick
an anaphylactic darkness
midnight's philosopher
deepens us thus
to difficult blue

Being Human

I am reading Rumi
reading Tu Fu
and thinking of being human

last summer
Marty and I
slept in the farmhouse loft
under French heaven near Vitteaux
and we lay in our separate cots
like boys at camp
laughing, talking silly
making fun of everyone
we were mostly ourselves, middle-aged men
with the window open
to starlight
and the evening breath of the fields

look up at the slant of ceiling
the slant of beams
this room was built
for dreaming
and we were giddy as lads
with happy lives, not
old Tu Fu, his sadness settled
like shadows, like rivers
like cold stones of winter
and the bitter darkness of long nights
and the lonesome insomnia
of small hours
like the mystical beauty of death and dying
and the inescapable anger of the soul

our hearts
refusing the silence
with a lovely slowing exhalation
as we each become
more pensive in
the loosening limbs of slumber
relaxing our hands like unfurled leaves
and pressing our faces to linen

meanwhile great rivers of the earth
the Tigris and Euphrates
the Yangtze
the Amazon of my father's last days
flow on
and what would I buy
from the famous floating markets of Bangkok

I would purchase the rains of remember
I would purchase the stars of recall
and what to preserve in a poem
but the drenching of darkness with light.

One Leaf in the Breath of the World

Many the Wonders

This morning over coffee we laugh
with the sun in the east
as ever-yellowing sky
and I read aloud
how a man in a fast sea flea
was drubbed
and drowned by a duck
with the man in the water
and the duck on the wind
an odd convergence
of flight and float
as with the low migration of death
by brain-bone and wing
the man went suddenly dull and dumb
to the world to be struck
and he sank from himself
as the soak of the soul
went wide as a shade-washed wave
wide as water weed
uprooted by a bottoming engine
and the sheriff confirmed there were feathers
plumed to the shine
as if the machine were an egg half-born
the careful sheriff
carried the word *duck*
found as a full-tongued flavour of feathers
in a dead duck-hand like a soft-mouthed dog
and he delivered the news to the shore
that we do not die always as angels
no, some of us go to amuse the cruel gods
who laugh like the feeding of fowl
when the hungry
mergansers are begging for bread
and what passes for mourning is mirth...

The Horses of Bethany Hills

The horses of the Bethany Hills haze
are grazing on the scorched grass
the appaloosas, the palominos
the five-hand browns
four in the faded paddock
twelve in the maple shade
standing in the grey stain
whispering
their long tails brooming the heat
one lone mare
wanders out into the small valley
in among the yellow splash
of the lasting birdsfoot trefoil of the dry meadow
tough weeds
melting along the path
like buttering the bees
under the ugly crow guard
that caws the murder
warning that man is walking
overclose
with nothing to hold him
but the mood of morning
nothing to drive him away
but the need to be doing
while the songbirds chirm by the houses
where wind-obedient shadows slim
and wave him on
with their sketchy circles, singing.

Undressing the Angels

such pageantry in this
to set aside
the failing energy of wings
the floating feather shadow
like the slowing slave fan
of an ancient evening sleep
this stirring fall away of darkness
and of heat
a measured loss
a disappearing bird to set inside
the blue belief of dreams

and then, the ring of light
the luminous and radiant affair
like water vowels of a brilliant well
the burning wish
the iridescent whispering of O
come briefly to the fevered breath
in smoky shapes of scintillating dust
what holds the summer moon
holds this
full circled in reflecting mist

and then
the simple gown
like fog in wind
the thinning haze that shades the sea
regard the bluing dawn
the clarifying dusk
the unshaped frailty of infragrant white
the pearl we make of night

and what we want of angels
angels want of us

the vanished touch
the tidal heart
the single hurt of being here

Mustn't Complain

delicate as thread fray
the insect
born in winter
hovers within
the lift and fall
of his own weary-winged
will

knowing, if he dare
to land
on the snow-grey
edge
of wet things thawing

that he shall
surely die

while the poet
at the window watches

the rain
throws dreary quoits
on white ice

and one life
disappears.

Operation Yellow Bird

In 1959, the Ocean of Wisdom
the Dali Lama
disguised as a soldier strolled
into the outer darkness
the world beyond Tibet
with a rifle slung upon his shoulder
like the individual burden of war
slumping him a little, the leveling of bones on bones
like the weight shift of a bundle in a boat
a water-dizzy equilibrium we feel
as it is with fear for life in us
when the heart double skips and sinks
on the wrist like a small blue stone going still

and he walked like the blur of sleep
in the starry gravity of the night
and he laughs to tell it now
how he was blinded
as with moon mist and river fog
some poets will compose the light half seen through cloud
that little flickering of joy
caressed by shadow cross
the wick that grips the memory of flame
the smoke that drifts like dream
the inner glance and
all.

Elegy For Al Purdy

the blue heron
stands alone
on one leg
knee deep in the black bay at Coots Paradise
his solitude and studied stillness
like wind-and-water-weathered wood
the broken barkless bone-brittle elm
that sank itself
all but for this
the last and lonely
leafless and unliving branch
thrust up and lighter
for the visible half-movement
when the hard-to-believe-in grey-eyed thing
he is becomes a bird
as it turns the lean curve of its carved head
like something rocked-on walking
to show an underwater will
from step-weight on a nearby stone
and then
he spans his wings
and shatters off this boggy shadow glade
like stain on startled glass
and he's buoyant in the blue
and big
enough to carry twice the darkness
by his leaving
these little stolen day-lost
silhouettes of drifting night dropped down
and grown ever-larger farther as they are
until he lands again
outside the lead-sketched light

and in wordless height of draft
becomes the thought of *loft*
and what it is to be
both object and metaphor
all mournful
and uncapturable as wind.

One Leaf in the Breath of the World

Woman, in a dream of desire
I have come to your shy mouth

left it wordlessly shining
like a silver scar

found the silence of sighing
that suffers the moon

I have seen how the bud
in the natural pear
goes grey as an ash
in the blossom's result

how the heart might quicken
like apples in August through autumn

and also, the stillness of sorrow
and also, the trembling soul

      one leaf in the breath of the world

The Silence of Secret Singing

the teacher
is standing in the playground
when a little girl
she doesn't know
runs up
and hugs her hard from knee to shoe
and looking into her down-turned face
chirps *I love you*
then races away
like the flittering of a shrub sparrow

this heart
that has no home

The Semi-Permeable Rain-Soaked Tent of Sleeping

What a dream's exchange
are we
you take the quiet walker
I'll take the flying child

the moth in the room
and the moth
in the mind
are the same ...
to hear the floorboards creak
like lumber curing in the heat
when the house in the rain
is real
or the flightless rising
of window-leap
like a wind-caught leaf let loose
watching as from shadow-cast
of canyon crows drifting
a darkness that lightens the light
to wake up believing
we've been
with our backs to the source of an actual blue

to float
from the bed
like feathers on breath
though pillows seem portable stone
what whispers the pins
of each word
we might use
to say we were there in the true
like ova of wings to the full of the shell
like dust
when we sing on the floor.

Blackout Thursday

last evening we went walking
the uncommon quiet
where people were drawn outdoors
into the perfectly powerless
newly arriving urban darkness
pouring like engine oil
flowing out among
the brilliant energy of stars
and everywhere
neighbours crowded in conversations
upon their postman's porches
and we could easily overhear
the talk, and also
the lazy thwick of basketballs
finding the earth
between fathers and daughters

and I imagine
a hundred poets, perhaps a thousand
listening and musing in pencil movement
and taking this test of the human
what under audible birdsong
becomes the re-acquaintance
of murmuring voices
like rock shallows in rivers
and what gives important pleasure
in the only slightly less luminous
cul de sacs and boulevards
avenues and mostly gentle streets

will be lost to us again
when the lights come on.

Swearing in Church

We're sitting to supper
at the baby sitter's house
when her parrot
begins to squawk

goddamn kids! goddamn kids!
  goddamn kids! goddamn kids!

and at this refrain

her parrot cursing
like a pirate's shoulder
perseverating on disgruntlement

goddamn kids! goddamn kids!

our hostess
blushing like beets water
forces a smile
that says

how sharply quiet
the taxidermist's fox
how ornithological
the permanent stilling of beaks

and she throws a glance at the perch
as if the bird
might learn about silence
from knives in the night.

Walking Bethany Hills Approaching Devil's Elbow

Here where the glaciers
have scumbled the land
where the hills come
graveling down
to the slow-to-walk geography
of human roads
no man is tall enough
among these old moraines
to see above that sounding
to the clouds
and closed in by the rolling
to and from
the rise and fall
of estuary ice
and all the other accidents
of time's retreat
I small myself
and sojourn to a stillness
where the Pleiades
have lithely leaned
like poplar daughters
laundry hipped
and talking of the day.

And if the wind
should wind my watch a little then
and set the summer going
might I cling
to the blade of the hour
as does the stick-brown bone
and may I mark the milkweed's state of mind.

My Son Swatting at Bats in Costa Rica, early evening

a bat fevers above us
twitching in the torpid tangled darkness
convulsing like leaf shadow
a torn away tawdry fraction of evening drift
he swoops and rises
gleaning a thready swarm
lessening a delicate hum
with a sharp-faced appetite
performing a disobedient glide against gravity
and the haphazard
or your hands which swat empty air
against the will and dignity
of courage—you are suddenly
flailing at indifference
as he flips and flaps like a broken bumbershoot
a cheap black umbrella
a widow's parasol
something a clown might lose
falling from a tightrope
his big shoes
battling the laughter
into a self-ridiculous afterlife ...

The Fifth of Four

every day at five p.m.
four pelicans arrive
in flight above the Costa Rican ocean
where my son has been
riding the waves for hours

they swoop and land
and lift and fall upon the swells
the waters rise and rest
like sheets flung out to breathe upon
the gentle mother-making of an evening bed

these water birds
attend the surface
floating up and down each crest and trough
my son, the fifth of four
the only one who cannot fly
his round intelligence inhales the salted air

where wishes crash
and stingrays stick and leap
like dampened kites

those four companions seem
as ancient in their shape
as some Jurassic thing
descended from the lizard winged
and laccolithic time

comes foaming in as endless
as my father watch
I see his precious head
beside those creatures come to fish
the tide's arrival

each night the moon's a broken
gourd that will not carry water well
though it lift
entire oceans up
and hold me in a buoyancy
like recent thoughts of gone-dry mars

Mulberry Song

in mulberry season
my grandmother's bedding
hung on the line
catching the mauvening wind
full sail
under the purpling gluttony of grackles
caught singing in swaths
so her sheets filled
to the violet splash-hem with guano
like the virgin pride of Portuguese brides
flagging their colour
in ruin and ravished by
favours of love
what once had been white
was smocked to the edges with seed
and all the sweet result
stained the appetite
of starlings with the hunger of song

I too have thrilled
to climb crushed fences to set
my voice alive among brilliant berries
to seek the pluck
and throb of tremulous response in branches
to feel those delicate polyps yield
my fingers faintly stained
like a ink-maker's passion for bishops and kings

why was my grandmother
angry at birds
her laundry made livid in that liquid breeze
like sad sailor's shouting for shore
when the water
lies crimson for miles

I favour such blush
the feathered purlieu
she comes to with axes
and ladders
to sunder the wind and to trim
wild places away
such a forest
she sharpens to silence
by shaping a billowing whisper of bleach.

The Vanity of Grackles

the grackle walks
the wet circumference
scribes the wide green oval
of winter water
in the pool
with feet like a vine
plucked at the twig ends
of what makes autumn wine
from absent grapes
and he flutters into splashy thirst
couples with the brief illusion
of a second self
slakes a feathered flight
and he keeps the company
of blue-capped starlings
and blood-breasted spring
all come to solve
a grey perimeter of sad cement
the surface sunk four inches from the weight of light

this liquid window set
into a frame of garden ground
holds out the weed bouquet
that courts the deeper damp
beneath where mayflies swarm in clouds
like casual conversations
exhaled by blurs of human smoke

what vanishes
when he is gone
pulls at the threadbare hem of thought
lets out the length of things
the soul
that fills the fool
like blowing gloves
to fit the hand
or shaking socks for feet
we are become the windy washline
of ourselves
we fill our clothes by drifting past
we are what happens to the darkness
when you fill the vase

we wait
the blooming blue
the spray of stars
the nest beyond the water tree.

Smashing the Sparrow

for weeks
the sparrow had worried the window
as if to say
I'm also in the glass
and can't get out
of the lacking...
oh see those stone birds
on their garden baths
I'd wash them real
oh see the delicate columbine
the butterfly visits
the hummingbird thrills
and yet it breaks to be touched
I'd lift it from fracture
like a song of straw
like a thread I'd sing
beyond the button weight
of broken hearts
that do not winter well
But when the sparrow fell
three children came
to smash it into feathers with a brick
they dropped so hard
it broke the walk beneath
three boys out larking
and looking to find the surfaces of hate
arriving at the easy evil of us all
they charmed the gizzard
with too big a rock to grind the seed
a stone the spirit could neither lift nor roll
though cantilevered with a three-day awe
and then strong nations dripping fire
did not pause though one less sparrow
broke its beak against eternity.

My Lost Sister
for Jane, 3 hrs. old

a single goose
is grazing grass
like a drowsy-scissored seamstress
dozing in her work

I want
that pluck sound in silence
that quiet snip of locket wisp
my younger sister   never lost
though
she died a child

The Fourth Sparrow

How like a basement apple
is my love
how like a too-ripe plum
an autumn peach
a winter grape, an apricot indoors

let others praise
the long monotony
of the bodiless soul
the spirit suffering
the discontinuous softness
of memory as momentary touch
when bones are but
a broken branch and we're withering
above the ribs like wood smoke
heavening from a distant hill

meanwhile
I will romance the inner appetite
the sacred silence
of a lingering kiss
the three brown sparrows
of my singing heart
have taken flight
the one direction where
they fail to go
is where I am
and waiting.

What Suffers Into Shadow at the Edges

Listening to the high
loud carpentry of birds
building their bug holes
hammering home
an appetite in the altitude
I am reminded
of a busy and beautiful silence
I have not heard for weeks
oh what a lovely rattapallax
above the shingles
of these shelters
with their chimney smokes
dragged grey
with light after rain

everything this April almost Easter
rises wild brown
and heaven fits the sky
while the lonely woodpecker
frames his natural cross
from pileated pine
in this water-flattered gloom
what suffers into shadow at the edges
might suffice

The Lost Hawk

they threw a blanket
over the lost hawk
sitting like an ornament of the age
on the car's high chrome
disoriented by downtown
he'd been hunting ledge pigeons
percolating among
the public buildings, midst the uptown things
the gargoyles, the friezes, the low stone lions
of inner city postal service

these living feathers
quiver to be caught, quiver
like ancient quill-penned poets
tensed to the pause of their breathing ink
touched wet to the blot-point of it, emboldened and
predatory as the black eye
of a terrified bird
bringing its beautiful swift-winged hunger
to the page, to this slab-coloured wilderness
and the falsity and confusion of artificial nightfall
hooded by comfort like a kitchen parrot

what and where
does he believe himself to be
bronzing as he is
into a difficulty, the lackluster
ambergris of this smothering two-handed darkness

the same we use to tuck
our children in
to stop the fear of dreaming with

The Beauty of the Birdless Cage

See what a lovely thing
I have built
with bent wire
how at the open door
there is such an otiose swinging out
for an emptying inward
of no thing
only the fine-ribbed shadow
of shadeless light
bearing the weight
of weightless waves
of curved and motionless darkness
only clock-touched time, untrapped
by stillness throbbing silent hands
sweeping a sorrowing absence
like the tearloss of the dead

what trembles among tall grasses
what sings in the red-hearted heights
what feathers its wings
in the full shrill gloaming
of bird loud summer
under the silk-hooded blue
of heaven drifted grey
for the flickering freedom of stars
going *arrive arrive*
as they're leaving

what distance is this unto midnight
what dream's companion
of unseen passing

must I close my eyes to contain
such glowing
such vanishing into the real

Talk of Trees

I sit in the city park late in the day
and alone with autumn
watching the poplars
spin their yellow leaves
in the wind
they rattle there in the thousands
and go still, rattle and go still
as heaven darkens down
like the dimming to grey of a huge blue-roofed room
and Bruce comes by
walking his small dog
and we talk of these particular trees
how important simplicities
have become
as we age in the sound of the wind
with its voice of evening
fathering the far edges of everything
like the whispering secrets
of lost gods
who cannot find the words
for where they are in the world

and the leaves twist and turn
like the fixing of time
to an imprecision
with a windy aspiration of shadow say

and I am arriving at the true interior quality of light
where it touches the darkness of the heart
like memory and dream
and Bruce asks me, "will you write of this"
and I say, "no, not of this"

Adoration of the Unnecessary

Seiche—Long Point Bay, Port Dover

often in the dead calm of a motionless morning
when the lake is smooth as pulled silk
polished blue with a new-washed sky
shining like a carried mirror
with the still reflection of waist-deep bathers
afloat in colours pooling away from their bodies
like rainbows of wet oil
it comes at first as a long line
far out in the fish-deep waters of Long Point Bay
a linear pulse
visible as if of a counterpane
undulating about the dream sigh of a water god
followed fast by shore hush
wave on wave sounding the drag of sand and shell
and the waders respond, briefly rocking where they stand
like the thought toddle of lost equilibrium
and also of an evening
I have seen this same windless oscillation
curling its lip in the harbour
nudging docked boats
so they bob and joggle
like the last swirl of exhausted dreidels
dizzy with the loss of turning
somewhere in the deep shallows
of felt beauty, well below
the ghost's slip of the coming on and the going away
of ephemeral mists
there resides in me, the true possibility of my soul
its memory alive at the very tuning fork
of Adam's resonant bone
receiving life and responding in kind
to that breath of grace

Wild Blue Caterwaul

a plague of grackles
swarmed in a vaporous drift
threading the pine
with a loud squall
of black noise, briefly
taking its rest
in the high conifers
of morning, ten thousand birds
tuning their voices
in one awful orchestration
like an artful madness
come to the mind of music
what timely choir
I borrow against stolen silence
and the occupied quiet
arriving by way of this caterwaul
at the contemplative kinesthesia of fingertips
each with its cuticle moon
heart-lit by warm sundogs of darkness
and blood-white
ascension with a luminous arc
at the root of the nail
and all is life proving
where the whirlpool of the soul
might touch through from within
caressing the language on this page
to be the memory of wind
where the torn leaf rages

Briefly Beautiful

on the trail
I see the lone road duster
lying in gravel like a small stick
earth-coloured
fragment of a snapped branch
resembling a filthy twig
a thing my little dog
might worry in his mouth
like he's cracking the marrow
from short bone
toss, toss, and it's done with
broken and tested and done with
but—suddenly
black wings unfold
in short flight
and the Carolina locust
breaks free like flame from kindling
and is briefly beautiful
landing and folding inward
again reforming the drab insect
no longer lovely, becoming
the saw-faced bug
though it was for the briefest while
momentary butterfly with the watered silk
of its jet-and-yellow fringed wings
now closed away like a shut and buttoned fan
watching the shadow I cast in the day
nearby and knowing
I too depend upon luminous darkness
I point at my heart with a walking stick
and hope my heart knows I am here
giving hand-some alert
to unseen and unseeable wings

Solving Sarah's Riddle

The little girl
out in the green darkness
catching the light
for her luminous jar
sings to herself
"we catch fireflies
 we don't catch bees
 we don't like bees"

and her grandmother
laughs
to think of how
we carry the sky
in our minds
when we're young

so we might seek what is found
in the flower-hipped flavour of words

I saw
where night fell to ditches
at the mud-edged hour
of evening

and what a beetle-bright
heaven it was
that glowed
through the weeds at my feet
like the burning of starlight
through dreams
too old to remember
too new to forget

Watching Two Cormorants floating on ice in the lake in late January

it is mid-winter
and I am standing
on a high clay overlook
watching two night-black
waterfowl
riding the mealy rhythms
of lake waves
in the rise and fall
of a wet grey world
arriving and re-arriving
at the white rot
of an ice edge
this being
the cold transmutation
of a coming in and a going away
of a well-soaked measure
a stowing of solids
and a pouring off
from one sharp *describe* of fatal shards
shattered at the muscled arc
of a splash
this glassy place where the dive seems
most brave
these cormorants
locked in the gelid up-slosh
of that slow design
what holds them there
at heaven's hunger
with the will of themselves
to be themselves
for as long as the weather lasts

Master Dogstorm

my little dog shivers
cowers, hides
makes himself small-in-the-shadows
a quivering lump in the bed skirts
indivisible from the floor
he vanishes
like a chastened child
sobbing and shamed by
the stormy ratapallax of the window
arguing wind against glass
the borborygmus of dark weather
rumbling over the grey belly
of the lake beyond the yard
lying in the lonesome corner
his body completely still
as though touched by the palm of death
he holds his breath
and counts
the watery lashes
at the coming on of rain
feels the wet gush of the downspouts
the shuddering footsteps of thunder
thumbing the ribs
through the broken spine of the house
his heartbeat
pushing the dome of his spiked up fur
to the limit with its caged red fist
shouting—I want out, I want out—
like the attic madness
of a phantom locked in a trunk
and starving for light

and he looks my way
when I find him
his sad eyes
accusing me of being the sole cause
for to him
I am the bifurcated god of all pleasures
and all pain
I am all things essential
I am the blue resolution
of this overcast
and he seems to wonder
why I am withholding the quiet
why am I
bringing on this loud
and relentless phantasmagoria
of noise and light
when with a simple wave
of my powerful hand
I might calm
the cruel-to-dogs barometer
but for now
he is cringing in the please-don't-find-me regions
as though I were touching a slow match
to an unavoidable boom
snapping the sparrow bone
of his spirit
even when he is dead
he knows he will be afraid
as the dead are always afraid
when the life in them
is something other than life

Feliz Navidad

tonight we watch the winter fireworks
from along the cliff above the bay
and listen to the locked-in agony of dogs
that lovely awe-struck spray of light
that blooms against the backdrop of a blackened sky
each boom in subsequence has consequence
next door the cats climbed curtains to the rod
and the Chows were cowering in the closet corners
like the fear we sometimes feel of thieves
I thought of Whistler's *London* as I watched
as in the gallery of God
the moon and stars
came clear against the roaring engines of the absent sun
some pyrotechnics popped like musket volleys
at the harbour's smoky rim
some thundered in the heavens
like the guns of ships in siege against the shore
and after that cascading fountains
sparked the sky
in festive reds and Yuletide greens
or trailing trails of white
that fizzled into twisted ribbons as they hissed
meanwhile the rockets of the Hezbollah
take lives in old Jerusalem
and in the Gaza
the living learn to loathe the source of death
as in my neighbourhood
dogs warn dogs against the ways of man

Contemplation of a Dead Loon
on the Beach at Long Point Bay

on the beach
a dead loon rots
into rubble
one wing fanned over
an otherwise open face of stone
the small break
in the voice of the bay
builds a wet dune wave by wave
against an anonymous cairn
while the flesh
of this avian body
vanishes leaving only
beak and bone
the quill-sharp face
the wing still feathered
like an overlarge shuttlecock
in shadow flight
downward, think here
of an Italian mask
crafted by masters
of black wax
and slow darkness
a wet-fingered snuff
of smoke withering
to linger like threadbare linen
blinded by time
and somewhere
far too late in the day for lamentation
mournful silence
gathers to an afterthought
of empty water and sand grain
silting as though
with the shallow breathing
of someone sobbing as they dream

In my lonesome craft

from my lonesome craft I see
the luminous surface of the still bay
shining an indefinable green
undulant and wimpled
like the heat-grey cooling of burnt steel
unscrolling in blue light
and everywhere dappled
by the inconsistent chiaroscuro
of an indecisive sun
on this cool-warm shadow-active day
where I am buoyed
by the boatstain of my slow reflection
moving to the hollow knock and drag
at the drip-edge of my paddle

I let myself glide
as I glance and look
and watch and sometimes see
the yellow spackling
of butter-coloured single-cell algae bloom
coagulating as a swirling river
meandering in the proof of my wake
like the oil of thought
words might change our thinking by

and in the afterglory
of my lazy hour
on the lake
I stand with neighbours on the cliff rim
at the overlook

and we discuss
the chemical traceline
seeming a sulfurous corruption
ghosting the keel-cut at the stern
of my long canoe
coming this way home from the harbour

we are defining how
we might comprehend
by shallow touch
the briefest momentary meaning
of the heart
beneath the bone
holding a palm-line to the dark drum
of our own and only
unseen and unseeable self
wondering also
how in the deeper regions
the sand bed
might know the presence of the light
as being there beyond the reach of light

wherein what downwells as warmth
also washes the shore shells
and dimples
the sand by weeping away from splash
like the rain-worry of a failing storm

I am this opaque vessel
this rock-bellied vase
this volume
dropping its thirst through a long silence
to a quiet promise where this voice
becomes a dry companion
to what the water says

Desire on the Wind

it seems I am waiting
for the perfumed sails of Cleopatra
wafting with desire on the wind
from the blue seas of the soul
what burns in the bones
but the beauty of being
or loosens the limbs
but the plunge and the play of light
in the green-thinned leaves
of an August breeze
what copulatory dawn flares on foam
what star-seeded
fertility of night in the dark
blooms black-ripened by dream
as she
arrives in her slave-oared ship
on the shores
of morphia and her moon-pulled
waters deepening
under the keel, waking
the language of waves and
of arms and the slow red voice
of each dead man's heart
with the spade heel
who opens the earth
with old involving
puts a doctor's thumb
to the still pulse
a silver brilliance
to the breathless mouth
an ear to the bell in the oak
and the golden honey-fragrant
hip of a sheet with its flowering
hive in the roof of a cave
where the wild bees work in their comb.

Modeling Borrowed Swimsuits
at Christine Shinohara's House

we were young and
you were modeling borrowed swimsuits
at Christine Shinohara's house
and I was watching
lost between the interests of the body
and the pleasures of the soul
thinking, I confess a loving
of the bounty of the water's bright caress
how it deepens colour in the cloth
like butter-darkened silk
where it dampens in the wave swell of our being
we are shadow-stained illusions
of illuminated dream
in the sweet touch of a much-imagined sea
you came into the room
umbilical beautiful
white-bellied by winter
or modest by turns in fuller-fabric suits
your warm and naked little feet
left blush lines on the polished wood
like the sand-vanished walking of a drying tide
and we were going away together that first time
going south to the sun
ten sleeps to the day since then
ah wife, how time remembers
all unenduring things
in the last unlasting hour
of the milk-shade of the moon
and the slow match
journey of a dying star
burned backwards into distant black
an older inanition than the days of light
meanwhile within the branch droop of our bones
we seek a wiser tree to find
what love reveals

Adoration of the Unnecessary

this morning my wife and I
were reading
in the lake-room
while the wind-dappled play
of light and shade
upon our minds
alive with the language of pages
insisted itself
on our attention
shadows blooming and vanishing
where illuminated darkness
briefly stained the paper
and was gone like wet splashes drying
and it seemed
like the flicker
of sunlit water
there in the shallowing deep
centre of the lovely
good-hearted warm
of two lives

Evidence of life lying in the sand on the Atlantic shore of America near Hampton north of Boston ...

I contemplate a photograph I have made
as framed by human footprints fanning out and away
from the shallow impression left
by a small dog also padding through
surrounding a tangle of rope
looping like offal abandoned
from the gutting
of a water beast
blue and yellow and aquamarine
chord with one woven through
the ochre hue of powdered blood
but mostly jute or hemp
knotted and balled up
in a thick ess
casting a ragged shadow
like beach grass in sunlight
all of it caught in wire mesh
this viper's nest
braiding the beach
like the dirty white worming
umbilicus of things once
put to a seemingly greater purpose
imagine then
the shop spool wound
with new cordage
as from the rope-maker's best day
measured by the yardage
of a fisherman's scarred arm
that strong meander of story leading here
to this shipwrecked bricolage

those footprints long since washed smooth
by the incoming tide and windswept
as though by these words
whatever is meaningless under God's eye
I wonder
though it is certainly not this moment, not these eyes

Nymphae

Imagine this

...the living imago
of your lovely form is born

orange Nymphae
of the woven womb

set there within the delicate cradle of your chrysalis

two straining wings
grown velvet-wet
within the fragile fulcrum of the soul

we who are heart-haunted
adumbrated by a gentle itch

with hands to quell
brief darkness
and the death of stars
might marvel
at such windless monuments
of momentary light

though now, we also wash the world in oil
to smell
the fragrant ooze of stones and dying water birds
dark angels blackening the shoreline
while we dream
brave God who made us
with His mud-measured thumb
perhaps He weeps to wash His guilty hands

Toad

there is a toad
living in the dry earth
in the hollowed-out darkness
of a faux lighthouse
a place I'd rubbled up
with lake stone shaping a rocky shore—
wet only by rain
which lifts the fan relief from a petrified fern
as it is with the tongue of a child
who dampens a fossil
or spittle on granite
what deepens the red on washed brick
or waters the mica
so it glints like the quick glitter
of isinglass squinting in slate
what's there holds the rotting struts
and the crossbeams punk to be touched
and the tungsten in the globe
has burned itself thin so it shivers
like dust on the whisker of an old cat sleeping—
when I move the unsound structure
ugly toad blinks
and hops
once—then stops
where he is
suddenly homeless
in the shadowless heat
his flesh like a lump of river mud
you'd grip for pargeting a hole
what good is the soul in me then
if at the blind edge of blue hydrangea
this quick stillness
fails to build a green haven, also
for toad-hearted things

Beyond The Seventh Morning

night sky to the east seems
faded black by the stray blush
of beach lights
so
I walk west along the sand
into star-dazzled darkness
arcing over the lake
with all the obvious astronomy
burning its belt
in the big water
and I dream the good fortune
of ancient amazement
when staring
into the prehistoric predicament of midnight
ancestored by moon-veils
and planetary awe
in the sleep shadow
of a loud fire
in the sound-zone
of a lonesome heart
I too
mantled in the far gaze
might find
my story there
exactly where it stops
to tell itself
the time

Oh Be My Most Strange Valentine

eight doves at rest
perch on the naked
black-bark branches
of a winter maple
all of them buxom, fat
voluptuous, as though floating upward
with feathered breasts
swollen like the last ripening
of weightless fruit
resting under heaven
grey as chalked slate
the sky filtered with cloud
like lamped gauze
with the perfect burning circle
of our own solitary and forever-lonesome
white star
shining like the lenticule
of an apparatus
designed for God's
snow-coloured eye

Familiar

the geese fly low
above my head
so low
I hear the creak of wings
and breath
of feathers in the wind

the same late afternoon
four bluebirds
feeding on the cliff
their red breasts
swell the winter world
like fire
living in the ash
where otherwise
the world is grey
and weeds are dead
and burdock burdened
with its burrs
awaits a wandering of furs
to seed a patch
of barley clay
or welcome summer ditches
to a big-leafed green

White Lake Moon

this winter sun
barely burns
through a hazy scrim
of new-falling snow
it lights the waves on the water
in the bay
of the lake, the one the early people
called White Lake

and there is no old ice there
no deep striations
or ancient strata
to measure
Decembers before Decembers by

Here Where the Stone Remembers the Shell

the yard below the willow
is littered with winter limbs
osiers like battlefield bones of the fallen
and the snow rots away
in grey-white heaps of brown reveal
steaming at the edges
as though the earth were burning
how like the lustrum of young desire
in the land where feeling leaps
in the sweet regions of the body
with the lost heart
seeking the source of pleasure
at the pulse points
pleasure on the muddy shores
of this rain-greased morning
if we follow the cold retreat of mist
smouldering backwards from the rooflines
of these come-clear houses
and thereby see farther
into the fading knowledge of warming light
somewhere there is lovemaking
somewhere there is war
somewhere the great sea swell of a wave
swallows the sunken island
drowning the voice of doomed strangers
disappointed by God
and the fossils that litter the beach where I live
call out to the whirl of my thumb
still fragrant with the redolence of touching
the bone hollow of beauty
here where the stone remembers the shell
the leaf, the frond, the butterfly wing
the shadow of a final sigh of a breath
taken in and breath released
and forever releasing

Paper Wasp Nest

hanging in the naked maple
at the thin end
of a black branch
full and round
the paper wasp nest
suspended in the coming on
of winter
all autumn long
and well past December's solstice
clinging like the last remnants
of an over-ripening
until this very day
in late morning, with
the weather grey as smoke on glass
I mention to my wife
that I mean to take a photograph
before it falls
through that vacant air
between in-breath of earth
and out-breath of sky

but the gravity
that breaks the heartwood
away from the limb at the moment
of grip-cease
when loss outweighs
up-wish

And I Stare at Everything
in the Absence of Light

...Before the world awakens,
the quietest time
is the surprising shape of an O.
Empty yet full.

(a Glosa on Kate Marshall-Flaherty's poem "Pre Dawn")

Before the world awakens
in the dream-coloured dark
when I am most
mindful of memory's loss
at the quietest time
when my body
is heart-slow with sleep
and I almost feel
the shoulder rub of the soul
when it smoulders from within
like smoke from the wet burn of water-swelled wood
or the amorous exhale
of the best of all desires
when want responds to love
in the vowel bloom of grace
just before God's blue voice
announces dawn
in the surprising shape of an O
that crimson prayer
empty yet full
the writer
alone at an inner desk
his reverent attention
receiving first light like a better darkness
the one below the ink
impossibly perfect on the pure white page
in the held breath of unwritten moments
yet to come

This Is How We See the World

This is How We Sometimes Share the World

you must go one day to Urumbamba
the holy river of Machu Picchu
flowing through the sacred valley
of the Incas—this voice of waters
saying—*flat land of spiders*
in Quechua—saying itself
to itself in the shadow
of young mountains
in the ghost-green lee
of a thin-aired city of Cuzco
set there over the lean thrill of a verdant surmise
we traveled by bus below the *pataas*
fertile with harvest of May—for it was autumn in the Andes
terraced with *quinoa*
white-yellow heaps of maize, *papas blancas*
while old world words rise on the breath
like prayers
while women weave
the wools of an alpaca-fragrant dawn
in ancient patterns from deep in the mind
the cocoa-flavoured language catches all
blue-white snows of the black rock mountains
all   crimson drop-petal things
while cloud vapors
fade like cold blankets tossed down
over the peaks high above these drying grasses

A Life So Different from Mine

here he thrives
on the floating islands of Uros
cut from the black weave
of the buoyant roots of the *tortoa* reeds
severed from the life-giving plant
of the shallows of Titicaca
here on the big blue eye of the lake
he greets us from the green edge
of an anchorage—one of many
in this manmade atoll
standing on his small soaked acre
and where we walk sinks underfoot
like rain-softened wicker
he dwells with his wife in a wood-framed shelter
and is president of this world
where he lives a life so different from mine
it hardly seems a life at all
forgive me the hubris of gratitude
I do believe he loves his fate to be himself
proud and grinning in his colourful *chullo*
with his long-gun smile
taking a bead on imaginary waterfowl
he cries like the duck or the gull
in a song so real and true
it's a call from the very heart of the water

when I was a boy
and we were young and learning
we children tittered at the name
of that exotic mountain lake
hardly able to recall
the continent
we'd memorized its whereabouts
as with the oar plunge of a callow thought
we raced outside in busy gangs
like a herd come home
from the far pastures of evening
and there
in the random fortune of my accidental birthplace
I became
the gone-to-the-city farm boy
a bookish tourist
traveling the planet caressing the earth
like the darkening drift of cloud shadow
barely belonging where I am
I am everywhere
pierced by a self-proving light

Lalo's Walls

the proud Peruvian
professor of anthropology
our tour guide Lalo
perseverates on the quality of Incan architecture
pointing at the perfection of walls
in *Machu Picchu*
walls at *Ollantaytambo*
walls at *Racchi*
everywhere the great stones
fit at the seams and joints
like a leavening of bread loaf
rising together
some carved from granite
some carved from volcanic rock
basalt black
and brought from close-at-hand quarries
some from far valleys
what wonders he reveals of the ancient world
as he places a reverent palm
on the big-bellied curve
of a single seam
tracing the line of the bond
with the tip of his nail
like the natural path of a bead of rain

what a marvel
he says
see how they interlock
where they fit
this amazing masonry
crafted by the lost art of ancestors
knowing the solstice of the seasons
training its light
through the notch of a mountain
for the god of the sun
and the god of the moon
caressing these lintels like a lover's warm hand

he is imploring us
to pay a studied attention
to the distant past
he wants us to see where
the interstices held
even as the earth trembled
and scree boiled down from the broken slopes
of the high mountains
these walls stayed
stronger even than the monuments of memory
preserved by breath in story
while we stand and move stand and move
performing the work of walking shadows
timing the ephemeral darkness of a single day

The Last Supper

in portraits of the last supper
as they are painted
hanging on Catholic walls
in the cathedrals of Cuzco and Lima
the Peruvian artist Marcos Zapata has included
llamas, alpacas, the shy
vicuñas and
racing around the floor
at the feet of our Lord
and His apostles
the guinea pig
with Christ
breaking bread for the Passover
the roasted cavy
spread open on full display
from teeth to tail
on a platter set at the centre of a holy table
the sacred feast
also replete with uncapped decanters of *chicha de jora*
the local corn beer of the Andes
five thousand years in the making
that very morning
I had seen this furred rodent
racing over the floor in a woman's house
in a thick confusion of peeps and squeaks
under the watchful skulls of her ancestors

meanwhile at noon
I dined on guinea pig served in a restaurant
overlooking the market square of the city
my grandfather kept a sow and a boar
and a dozen pups as pets in pens in a barn
by his house in the town of my childhood
and I remember that vivid fragrance
of dung and lettuce and those peeps and squeaks
come alive in my memory
a friend of mine lost his own furry little fellow
in a puff of smoke
as he had let him run loose
unsupervised in the basement
where he had chewed through live wire
as rodents will when given the chance
as I turned the small creature on my dinner plate
for want of the meat
plucking the watch-work-delicate
bones from my mouth
I thought of all these things:
there are no guinea pigs in the Gospels
there are also no potatoes, nor corn
nor alpacas, nor llamas, nor vicuñas
how strange it would have seemed to our Savior
if the stone puma of these ancient people
had come to life and leapt in
through the open window
of the Eucharist spilling their shadows like wine

In the Colonial Regions of Lima

in the colonial regions of Lima
there are many abandoned mansions
architectural wonders of a wealthier age
with windows blackened by time
like dark ponds
holding under the white faces of the drowned
they are spectral and
cloud bloated with reflected light
now mere buildings
hollowed out by vacant echoes sounding
the gauzy scrape of wind-stirred spirits
emanations from empty rooms
where once
doyens of old-world aristocracy
floated through in flounces
like flowers tossed on an ever-tossing sea
important men
with business to do
on chain-fobbed days
with watch hands sweeping to cross the hours
like insects eating a meal of crumbs
these humans now
in the land of living light
haunt the streets
like the unborn shadows of evening

In the Catacombs
of St. Francis, Lima, Peru

I watch how the teenagers
dance and jostle
rub living shoulder to living shoulder
feeling the adolescent heat
and prickle of bare arms touching together
in the heart-warmed Eros
of their young bodies
the lovely girls toss their dark hair
some holding up their black tresses
some falling forward in waves
in a shadow-splash of beauty
the boys raw-voiced
the half-swallowed silent snow apple of the larynx
their new faces fragrant with the efflorescence
of cheap cologne
they all lean hard on the stone lip
for a closer view
looking down at the dust and bone
denizens of the catacombs of Lima
the ulnas organized in bins lying elbow to wrist
in a deep and dry earth-coloured darkness
the skulls like broken crockery
dream gourds of a city harvest
from twenty-thousand dead
dead some five hundred years
in that breathless basement

how time-tired
these lost ladies of Thanatos
these caballeros of absence
rubbled in heaps
like a crop of tubers
turned by a four-pronged potato fork

what sad lucubration
in the midnight melancholia of poets
might unlock
the ludic predicament
of thirty young lives
gawking with fascination
at the hermetic abundance of the dead

there exists
such an inescapable
lassitude
in these disarticulated heaps
like the lost
wine cellars of noble Lords
and petty gods
sour sipping the full lips
of these awestruck children
like dust on the breath of a kiss

All Too Often

the fibers of the alpaca come falling filthy from the beast
tumbling away from the ribs
in yellow smoulders like wet smoke
the fleece stinks of the fecal aromas
of grey-green mountain graze
it is stained by the piss of sleeping
in the camel slant of the Andes
high in the thin-to-breathe air in the Sacred Valley
where the fluvial rush of the Urubamba sweetens the earth
the *sacha Paraqay* root is grated into a foamy wash
to clean spun yarn
in Lima a three-thousand-year-old
shroud hangs like a hand-woven tapestry
on a museum wall this blanket for the dead
outlasting even the old weather of ancient gods
imagines the working fingers of the women of the loom
plucking the red music of the cochineal
the carmine-coloured wood louse
like the cut-throat crimson of the sun gone down
draining its blood in a rainless blue
all too often when we may seem real
even in unrecollectable dreaming
when the time-dry flesh of a dead king
shivers to be wakened like touched leather
as the bones come clear on the hands
like the shadow-crossed branches of night

Lords of the Gutter

no one gets near enough to touch
the stray dogs of Peru
which are sleek and well furred
and scavenging scraps
in the streets of Cuzco and Lima
none of them scrofulous
nor torn-eared
nor scarred nor fight ragged
nor patchy with ringworm
nor lousy with tics and itches
I saw no fog-eyed dogs
with lenses milky as beach glass
neither are they sick with heartworm
none car-killed
none crippled with ruined haunches
old and haggard and crooked at the hip
like humans
nor when I pass do they scatter
I imagine they must be descendants of royal whelp, bred
from the golden age of Phillip of Spain
for they have littered these road shoulders
with such a full-bodied darkness
I wonder if they are not dreaming
of when they'd once slept near the fires of Eden
when for them the past was not so very long ago
and their lives were less lonesome, less nameless

Golden Light of the Sun, Silver Tears of the Moon

if we moil in the morning
in the melting away of the golden waters of dawn
with our lips to the cup of the lake
in the unslakeable hour
at the breaking of day
drinking deep from the draft of far horizons
where the tall ships sail
going west and away from the light
and are heavy laden with the burdens of a foreign god
the stolen rooms come thigh deep
with idolatry of Spain and the old world
where night falls early
the sky cascading over Santiago
with a glittering wealth of coeternal stars
if then the moon weeps well over the ocean
bringing only its lunar month of sorrows
staining the face of woe
in the wake of our common grief
who am I dreaming in darkness
and who am I waking in light
from when my father last
shook his pocket coin
with wheat chaff spilled from his cuff
at the door in a golden trail of dross
wondering which do I value more
the golden light of the sun or the silver tears of the moon

YA—Now

there is a silence between us
where I carry your face
in my mind
like wet light
and there in dark fathomed
water of memory
I see that you
are an old man
being seen
by the traveller
taking in
the Taquleños Viejo
a Quechua elder with the weathered visage
of this village
overlooking the blue voice of the lake
in a distant land
and as I've carried you home
in my camera
I notice in bold black graffito
on a white wall
over your right shoulder
the single Spanish word *YA*
edged in ink
above the tousled shadow
of your boyish hair

and as I crack open the quiet moment
with the movement of my hand
I am reminded
of myself at sixteen
coming down off the train
to Moosonee
and walking among Cree children
selling stones to tourists
in the morning and of how
late in the day returning
to the station
I saw those same stones
scattered on the path

and if we value what passes between us
though we meet only once
what we might learn in the school of the soul
is there in the light
for the having

Counting Cranes

Mu—Not—lament
for the lost kingdom of I am

the lion gate
on my desk lies open
on the left—the leonine child
on the right—the world
and in the centre
my name
in pictogram and inkpot
I am at the invisible gate
of the forbidden city of Mu

I have set these jade creatures
on coasters bracelet brown with coffee stains
from the Silk Road
of Marco Polo
and I am born in the year of the rabbit
and testing the dragon of my luck—for it is March
the equinox a half-a-week away
on the Sunday of Purim
from the story of the book of Ester
celebrating the liberation from Persia
tomorrow St. Patrick will drive the snakes from Ireland
with a green thought

during the long weeks of Lent
in the sign of Pisces
coming into spring with its sad Friday
and the cruelty of the Roman cross

I heard today
a hopeless soldier
falling to his knees
in prayer at Anzio in Italy a ghost of battle
importuning "help me God, help me Father
do not send your son—
this is no place for children …"

and I am wondering
as I read a poem on the inner wisdom of objects

long after the mind gather
of this
solitary and most
singular incarnation

what anyone but I
will make of the meaning
of the bric-a-bracs on my windowsill
the stones and shell fragments
a vial of sand from wadi rum and beach glass
from Cuba and Korea and Thailand
—oh, the photographs, the sculptures
and flags of nation
will be easy to get wrong—

but the bricolage of strangers to my soul
I challenge with sunlight
pouring in like apple wine
that cruel to snow shadow line
marbling the ice with its grey patina
of chill moisture
like the wet windows of a cold frame
warming the seed bosom of frozen earth

and under the dormant russet
lies a ladder
fallen in the white froth of a filthy world
two feet in the air like a dead beast
a swollen step only the low fruit need fear
the lazy gather of lost gravity
equalized by the cruel energy of over-ripening
in winter's last hurrah

if the pencil maker
the paper maker and the poem maker
if only they could meet and share
one breath on the blank page and there
see everything I mean and everything I meant
my hand still moving and my hand is moving still
toward the light no longer there

A dream I dream
on my first night in Beijing

in a dream of my grandson
he is riding
the mask of comedy over the blue lake
a three-week-old infant
clinging to a gilded grin
little Euripides
the butterfly imago
shaking his spear
at the water

and I am standing on the shore
watching him drift
and glide and rise
and fall on the thermals
the old tragedian
unworried and laughing like summer
in the philosophical sunlight
of golden creation

and he
a small god
pale hero of moonlight
and morning

if I wake I know
he will remain in motion
until I sleep again

Is Beijing burning

we walk the smouldering streets
and cross
the smoky square
amazed to see
the ashy patina
that clings
to smudgy paint-shine
on the cars
the sun unseen within an amber sky
an artificial overcast
chokes all the light
our stars like fire hissing in an almost
combustible fog
the moment we burn
the edge of memory away
to find
the lie we'll tell
to children in their chairs
the future is a fuel to storms
today Chicago's blackened sky
today the water wall
that drowns a dozen islands
in a leveling aftermath
high winds that break the heart
and snap the bones to candle-crush

and there above Tiananmen
outside the lion-guarded gate
the face of Mao Tse Tung
smiling down through blurs of smog

what's truth to him
or truth to us
or truth to anyone
dishonest ghosts
with much to say
tell stories from the grave

A boy speaks of his childhood in the countryside outside of Beijing

as a boy in China
he speaks of how
he dripped liquefied wax
upon the wings
of a cricket as with
the weeping of that warm seal
he changed
the pitch and timbre of the wee creature's
song
oh sweet harmonious
singing of a single voice
like Emperor Zhu Di
who out of loneliness
carried for company
the insect in its cage
throughout his isolated court
the shrill-voiced insect
his only friend ...

as I recall
from childhood
how they sang among towels
chirping through ablutions
their small black exoskeletons
like warriors in armor
the sharp ideal
of their high-pitched music
falling quiet
as I came closer
to discovery—in mutual wonder

we two leapt
he like the black notation
of a shrieked vowel
seeking the corner cracks
of the room
I   like a kettledrum
booming for the open door

Undeserving blue

the one-armed legless man
his flesh tattooed by fire
lay like
a statue broken in the street by war
set there
for charity
beside his cup of coin

and then
along the tourist route
a second man
folded in and crumpled
at the chest
his body withered up
like winter fruit
a single head for sadness
emerging from the rot
as though he swam
and took his breath
above the grey confusion of half-set concrete

their handlers
bring them here
each morning
set out for shop and trade
jade lions
at the palace gates
below the smiling face
of Chairman Mao Tse Tung

at night
the guilty commerce
shakes a shattered hand
to count the take

and in the darkness
at the end of day

we turn a wheel of stars
to find ourselves
within the memory of God
our fate
defined by seeming grace, perhaps
or something less than true
in what comes clear to us
tomorrow as we wake
in undeserving blue

Tea flower falling

I touch
one fragrant tea flower
then watch it fall away
in sweet descent, to trace
the trail of its perfume
through aromatic wisps of pinkish light
unpetalling the air
with sweeps of delicate drift
undressing distance as it goes
tumbling down among autumnal greens
its sister seeds
remain to fix their season
in a winter stone
these hillsides wait for spring
to feel the pluck and hold releasing the grip
of the picker's inch of leaf
to find the palm-dried flavour
of an expert hand
the ancient skill
elixir of the learned response
how then to shade this language
with a faded word, one moment brewed
within the mind, a supple monument
that energy of joy and breath suspended
in the melt
come now home's common frost
to mother water from my weeping thumb
the window smears the scene
revealing all within the heart-warmed eye
we sometimes do our better looking with
to love the world half seen
beyond the self

too much to be enough
an all-sufficient glance of grace
when ice that's clarified by rain
becomes the rain come clear

Climbing the Great Wall of China

I climb the stairs
to where the great wall
breaks its spine
along the grey-green ridge
of smoke and fog above the Yanshan Mountains
and as I rise
I carry nothing more
than a shadow's weight of daily cares
and as I glance
I am amazed to see
how worn away by walking
are the stones
beneath my feet
how smoothed as though
by water over time
and leather trod
eroded by the come and go
of hordes of trekking solitudes
and as I touch
a single shape of chiseled rock
I feel the slave's fardel
the spirit burden of a broken life
the fragment of an empirical fear
the horse's heavy heartbeat
on the warring earth
the blackened hoof
that thunders on the steppe
with arrows singing
in a mind of troubled dreams

I pause
to let a lucky tourist
take a photograph
his friend
leans smiling as she breathes
to catch her breath
her bosom heaves *alive alive* and lets it go

I'm warm enough to wait a while
my quickened pulse
is like my father
at my morning door
it knocks to wake
an answer from my over-weary bones

and if he's there, or not
I rise
and seek the purchase
of a greater height than this

Counting cranes

at high noon
standing on the Bund
looking east across Huangpu River
at Pudong skyline
cast in grey smoke
as though seen through
the ripening lens of an aging eye
I think of the language of morning
when I talked over breakfast
with an American steel man
living here in Shanghai
since twenty years ago
in 1995 he said
half of the construction cranes
on the planet
were working in one city
meaning this new city
near the mouth of the Yangtze
in the financial district
all that I'd seen
the night before
illuminated and lovely
in the backdrop of an oriental night
dark and cast-iron black
holding Li Po's moon
like a sentry lantern
lit till dawn amazed by sleep
lost every artifice of light
and I remember
looking west and east
and east again
into that tall brilliance
dwarfing even the ziggurat
of ancient story in the rising voices of a broken world

when suddenly
a drifting scow
blackened our view
and like a knife in silk
the mind tore darkness to a plimsol line
from stem to stern
the ugly prow cut water so we rolled
upon its roiling wake
the shining city drowned in shimmering foam

if I say I prefer
the architecture
on the Bund
old Europe and her earth-brown brick
the commerce of a different age
less glassy in the gloss of time
the spread-wing gargoyle in the eaves
in flight through opium smoke
at the end of an era of war on war

what might the twenty-four million say

I've been to the Yu Garden
to the squat pagodas
and the natural stone sculptures
of a slower hour

and if my inbreath burns
like a dragon from the west
my outbreath also smoulders
at the river's bend building this poem
one scorched word at a time

The empty boat

when I see
the moon
over China

I cannot help
but recall

the lost life of Li Po

the drunken poet
drowning in a pond

the empty boat
a vacant afterthought
made more
buoyant by the absence
of the thinker
at the oars

how lonesome the light
without us

how dark
those brilliant beams

The Chinese on the moon

the news arrives today
informing this world
that the Chinese
have managed
to place a robot on the moon
sent out
into the myth of night
upon a fire ship
where science sets
its ineluctable eye
the powerful instrument
of the human mind
gone digging
through the frost-white rock
seeking sub-lunar soil
in deeper veins of unimportant dust
to find a thought of gold
the El Dorado
of the dark
empirical proof
of madness in the tides

from the menstrual crimson
of an oriental dawn
we take a breath of smoke
while glowing embers
of a burning star blink out

and blinded
by forgetfulness
forget again

I thought I was in China
held against my will

she says she did not fall
but rather
that she fainted, withering onto the floor

an old lady three days
slumped in clothing
like the nuisance of laundry to do

seventy-two long hours spent alone
in artificial darkness
lonesome for the light

and when she awoke

she said of her time
away

"... I thought I was in China
           held against my will ..."

her apartment floor in Paris
transformed to a locked cell in a distant land

her body
transported as though

truth in the mind
were the same as truth in the world

Suseok — viewing stones

my son, my grandson and I
were walking
the gravelly shores
of the Yellow Sea
on Daebu Island
looking west through amber sky
west to the entirely imaginary far-away
coast of mainland China
the sun
shining like a dulled brass gong
hung in soundless heaven
over the low-tide mudflats of Korea
and we were
looking to gather up
the most interesting stones
and only recently empty shells
the small cochlear conches
that hold the ocean winds of the world
as poems might hold
a meaningful breath
at the moment of deep-breath knowing

and I have gathered
my own little tea bowl
of chalk and silvery anthracite
carrying home the light of hope
brought here from these broken mountains
and that scaling off of iron oxide
from the water-loud coves
with their coming in and going away
of moon-drawn amplitudes
that swallow the road and drown the ankles
where the beach turns to vanish under
the afternoon drop-shadows
of the great engines of the sea

and as I hold council here
with silent beauty of granite
and pink rock
cobbled with dead creatures
who cling, barnacled
to the underbelly of a time-crushed
stratum and substratum
of cold vermillion

I think back
to the finding
when our three shades crossed
like the slow dampness of dragged black cloth

and there is this consolation to loss
the way memory
brightens
the shades and hues of meaning
like wave wash on dry rock
and tomorrow's freeze
that set the coast
in hard-white unwalkable shards of dropped ice

what we'd seen
beneath the heavy burden of winter
unpacking its load
on the threshold of a second morning
made everything
unavailable to the hands

but there
the heart reached through

An incident at the bridge of no return

in an assignment
involving a clear view
the young lieutenant
was trimming a particular poplar tree
so the Americans
might observe without obstruction
the deployment and movement
of enemy guns, and
training his axe
on the aspen with its shivering leaf
looking north
to the bridge of no return
he fell
from a fatal blow to the brain
from behind
the cold tool
blunting his last thought
like the dark wedge
where the burnt Y
of the barkless trunk
remains with its blackened knot
like a blind eye fastened at the fork
of two branches
it stands there
a scorched post crowned in rot
with us living on
in such
a ridiculous world
in the sad significance of risible things
where what matters most
seems valued least
and what matters least
is conserved
in the chiseled knowing of stone

The outset

at the foot of Gwanaksan mountain
at the outset of a wide trail
leading to the crags
and narrows above Seoul
where millions of city dwellers
take treks in the heart of the day
the sculptor Mr. Kim
has built a small house
at the gateway to beauty
and he sees us
stopping close by
admiring the poems
bannering the fence
in what to us is an unintelligible Korean script
and he emerges
comes to us, stalwart legged
a small sexagenarian man, smiling
strong in his bones
and he greets us
in a language we do not speak
grips us, with brilliant eyes
invites us in
to savour a morning coffee
black and sweet, fragrant
with the mildura of the burnt cane
of our common field

outside the door
a thousand hand-sized
Taegeukgi flags fly their four colours
in a winter breath
the red and blue

circumference a lovely circle
for uncomparing strangers
sharing the morning

he shows us
his own poem
a short piece on coming of spring
and the breaking of bread
by the chill
unfreezing of a snow-whitened stream

Timmy's down the well

as I am conscious
of the perils
of living in a world
that is bellum
and full with the falsity
of the fierce and terrible yawp of war
I send out
the kinder dog
of my most beautiful thought
and I am
wagging memory at important windows
I am barking
at the scriptoriums
of mad leaders
where oak drawers slide shut
on the keepsakes of life
I am howling
at the Lupercalia of a romantic moon
where light
and the mirror of light
are drawing in the muddy skirts
of my hometown waters
while the deeper ambitions of love
arrive and leave in waves
like the bridal bed
evenings and mornings
of warmed dreamers
who wake and sleep
in the swan tuck of angels

my son
who works and thrives
in government regions of Seoul
tells me
his school is at the epicenter
of the animosity of big guns
training their dark zeroes
at the soul of the city
and I know—
any sunrise
has its own Gallipoli
all moonsets in yellow air
might break shining glass
with a seismic whump of a great shattering
where we are all bad hammers
we are all
the pelt and pummel
of red stone and sharp sticks
on soft flesh

Mr. President
you with the burning tongue
take your crimson axe away
from my broken brain
I am here
singing from the common tree
among the magpies
among the crows
I come
palm line open to the blue ceiling

give the greater graves
the balm of a short shadow
I cast my longer darkness
onto the green recline
of an out-of-reach light
where we both breathe
we all breathe

and into this lasting language
of even the most ancient poets
I say, let Caesar weep
on the senate step
let him weep at the river
I refuse
the map lines of his desire
I bark
at the buoyant well holes
of my body
and am dangerous with a different
and far more powerfully resonant echolalia
of the resounding voice of a father's love

Broken time traveler

lying in the malodor of the midnight city
with our window open
to the burnt-black fragrance
of industrial winter
under sky's starless with ambient neon
of the urban neighbourhood of Gunpo
with factory smoke
drifting in from the fiery diseases
of commerce and labour
infecting the dream sickness
of this otherwise comfortable room
we are long married
and living
through the jetlag insomnia of broken time
we tumble together like river logs
in the cold inertia
of this new night
enduring the ennui of the deep-bone need
for sleep
at odds with the clock
and the grey gloom of a false hour

what asking there is, is
of the body
with its weird fatigue
the heart stumbles like a kicked drum
with its weakened want
to be doing
and doing again
that slow chore of its dutiful visits
at the pulse points
desire tapping its code
on the counterpane

if we are both awake too long
in the feckless melatonin
of an oriental dark
we are also becoming unwilling experts
of the bloom-light of dawn
the way it rises in the mind
like a waterline
the way it warms the glass
like wet ice
the way it suffers into the flesh
like the suffusing of a low-grade fever

saying to all the interfering exigencies
of sun-born day

get up, rise up
take up your bed and walk
into the great elsewhere
what waits is waiting
afterwards
there will be nothing to do
but   this

The insatiable hungers of the sun

my five-year-old grandson
is racing along
the low perils of a park wall
flapping his arms against gravity
like the wingbeat
of a flightless bird
and there on the parapet he feels
in this the common thrill of childhood
that is almost always
cruel with grandfather fearing
the knockout
and the shin bark
the scab and scar of it
the memory of bone break
something splintered
something cracked
something snapped at the green graft
that hurts in the cold

and yet
he scatters over the cinderblock ledge
blinking safely past the accidental blinding
of a bare-branched hedge
on and through
the white stumble of each snow trap
rising and running
over the dead groan
where winter heaps itself into a rubble of shattered ice

and he stops
at the high point
where he finally leaps
and lands
and climbs again
being the daredevil of this sure-foot carousel

until he's brought in close
by the clutch and giggle
of two schoolgirls
who fancy his big eyes
and the handsome dash
of all that male energy
wanting its name
they embrace him, lift him like a big doll
set him in motion
run and chase and are chased by
the big blue-bellied shadows of the sun on the snow

last night we were speaking of spiders

and how
they weave their webs
from the outside in
and I have seen them
drifting on silk
from tree branches
from windmill struts
from window sills
dropping down and fearless
like steel workers
lashed to high scaffold
swinging out
and seeking a second hold
a third, a fourth, a fifth sticky fastness
going clockwise in the sun
and catching the light
in silver strands
with beads of dew for the roses
the glass in my study view
is ghosted grey
like a handprint
after the hand has warmed the glaze
leaving like breath
that intricate silver lifeline
of the quick eight-legged lady

in Mongolia
there are fossils
ancestored in stone
from a million years
of continuous spider life
etched like burn shadows
formed by threads and buttons
from the garments
of lost children
however, after I wipe clean
all midnight evidence
or skein my broom
in the sticky whirl
sweeping the soffits and rafters
the morning comes
and she wafts against darkness
wins the cross weave
tattered with mayfly wings
and delicate filaments of brilliant dust
where things would rather shine
and be bothered by blur
frail monuments
that want my attention for the fuller silence

Going back to the world

my second son
finds himself floating
on the muddy mirror
of the Mekong
riding the big blue lung
of a foreign sky
in the remote regions
of Thailand
old Siam having her say
in the sultry voice
of a hot river stillness
when someone upsets
the boat
and he spills
laughing into the coffee-brown
shallows that gulp
around his body
like the pull on the line
of a smooth-bellied catfish
thrashing on a soft hook of bent light

and he uses that occasion
to dive down
to plunge his hand
into the clam-grip of the muddy bed
retrieving one wet stone
for his father
who wants only this thing

however unglamorous
however ugly
he wants

a river rock
or scree from a ruined hill
something a hen might swallow
to grind poor grain

a dull enough thing
not to be missed
by the mountain
nor mourned by the delta
nor grieved by the field

a dull enough thing
like at home on the lake
the glacial child of a big grinder
melting backwards
from the ten-thousand-year-old dawn
of an ancient
and even more primordial day than this

the fanned out energy
of a big crush
embossed on its facets
and bent at its curves

let diamonds and gold and silver
moil themselves
in the worm-heart of history
kings in their coffers
and other velvet-robed
panjandrums of the temple
the glint in the eye of a greedy council

his father
wants only
the privately precious dross
something marked by the local light
and culled
for lack of beauty but for this:
it was there
in the footstep darkness
of an all-ancestoring night
when empire rose and fell
to the silk breath of a dying counterpane
with maidens gathered in dew

my son knows
his father to be
just the sort of simple man
who like everyone
with a palm line
open to the alms of dawn
might wonder
at want and worth

*Traveling Through
Each Other's Lives*

Forgetful

here within this sand-white arc
of bent bones long-lost in the disinterment of a deep grave
at the sad moment
when the heart drops through
as on some archeological
grey-water gloaming
when heaven refuses the light loss
as it is with autumn's over-ripening
some winter orchard's
lassitude for the outlasting of medlars
this woman
in her island cerements
her skull bejeweled by a sacred stone
her forehead turned
to her mate
giving the halo-gaze
of love, the one she gave in life
the selfsame devotion, the quickening
that dimples the blue pulse points inspiring
the language of desire
how is it
that this pre-Columbian princess
has come to dust through dust
with this intact sombrelito
this capshadow of the soul
this small darkness
she holds
as a child might close
a half shell in her hand
the one she will find in the morning
and lose in the evening
forgetful of grieving

The Ungoable

it was the opposite of falling—
seeing her mother
waving from the shore
as she and her sisters
stood at the railing
of the ship
leaving Europe
after the war
her mother dimming
to a sorrowful deflation
a reified vanishment of love breaking the heart
the way the crag of a cove
breaks a wave
at the thin edge of the sea
one high sharp
exhilarating shatter-glass
moment of roaring
and sumping the rock hollows
to feel that unswallowable grief
the herniated ache
at the hiatus of an inheld sob
surely only a child
can hurt that way
yet I see
in the telling
how this lovely woman
relives the deep throb of loss
revivifying for the fraulein she was
born in Berlin
before the conflagration of the city
with its fire dead
immolated in the burning strasses

the Fuhrer sneering
through flame flowers
rising from the red garlands of his bones

the Swastika
blasted by sappers
crashing to the earth

lightning in the high branches
and the eagle kinder
of the Phoenix with no future

she mentions
a certain officer of the conquering Soviet
lusting after her mother
who was beautiful
and when her mother refused
his unwanted advances
he lined up her five children
placed a loaded pistol to each
of their temples
touching the muzzle
to the pulse point of each young mind
that black zero's cold metallic kiss
and then firing a single shot
in the air at the end, so she knew
the inescapable consequence
of a mother's refusal

and the same dignified
and much-loved mother
violated by the cruelty
of a choice
that is no choice

stood on the pier at the shore of the harbour
waving
her hand like the last glimpse
of the desperate drowned

those who are helpless in history
because they know by the needle of some inner compass
the ungoable direction of hope

On the Beauty of Being Elsewhere

I look out through
window glaze freshly frosted in last-night's snow
like the clinging there of new-washed linen
and beyond that glimpse
the sublimation of bushes
those fine-boned creatures
purified by winter
even where wind song
seems at this white hour
in the burning cold
overfull with sunlight calcified
like chalkstone—oh my Ontario morning
I am saying farewell
as I'm rising in the belly of this silver bird
emerging into a post-prandial blue
walking the humid torpor
of a Cuban evening
feeling the lovely melancholia
of being elsewhere

like a rose of ice
I water away
una rosa blanca
dying in the crystalline wave
Irish linen grown old
a snowflake on the tongue
of a child reciting Martí
amused by a poem he knows
as he knows in a moment
of ice and water
and water and sky's blue aspic
concealing the invisible flavour of light

One Morning in Mayabe

in the morning in Mayabe
a lone vulture
soars, kiting the thermals
the black flag
of his dropshadow
drifting echo-darkness over the mango groves
caressing the orchards by the lake
as though with the sorrowful breath
of a widow's veil—
we walk the hill
through medlars and soursop
the long leathering pods
of the flamboyant
rattling their saber sheathes
over the shortswords
of a wind on the march
as up we rise
along the donkey-dung road
to the finca casa of a reconstructed farm
there in the burnt-bean gloom
of a Cuban kitchen
Wency is doing the coffee dance
with mortar and pestle
and I am reminded how it was for me
making butter, churning in the milk slosh
of my own childhood home
as with the ache in my small boy arms
I felt myself
a drudge of the slow globulation
plunging the weight of a wooden cross
in turbulent oleaginous coagulation
of ultra-yellow coldering

clatter, lifting that stick from the suck
like curding and cheese clabber

what was that then
but the seemingly endless ennui
of a child's labour
and my mother
in time, gone butter black
a glossy tabula rasa
and I'm
a drone of dead roses
my heart
the stone of a busy hill

El Hombre con La Guitarra Azul

the man with the blue guitar
sings Martí
as we ride
the jaunting cart
horse-drawn along the sea-lit
lanes of Gibara, solo voce
"yo soy un hombre sincero"

and with wife
and friends in chorus
the song
in harmony lifting
over the buzz of shining strings
the melodious
mourning of the recent loss
of America's quintessential troubadour
of peace and source of song

that sky we see
is also star-subsuming blue
and this Jorge
with whom we share
a brilliant ear
one hour
in the cool grotto
a common cave
like the mind of the earth

two rock climbers
spider the wall
with handgrip and toehold

and float rope
and hang cradle
while three guitars
one mandolin
and twelve voices
flicker the candle of a distant room
as it is with the echolalia
of a much-remembered day

the priestly sigh at the end of service
the poet
breathless at the end of an overlong line
the lover
in pleasure, the child
in grief
and the eidolon of memory
saying hello and again hello

Broken Money "Bozuk Para"

if you live
in a land
of broken money, lost then
even
in a golden hour
of luminous darkness

under a white shard
of a sand dollar moon

that and
whatever chalkstone
crescent over Cuba
whatever milk-shell
fragment standing there
on the sea draw
of a great shallowing
a grand outwash
of a deepening elsewhere
feeling only that lonesome boatswell
of the heart's inhale
that undulant influence of mutable tides
at the soul of the ocean's imago
over fathomless trenches
where waves rise and fall and fall and rise
form and unform in foam flight
where luxuriant phosphorescent creatures dwell
alive in ultra-white ghost beds
of a great crush

if you measure then
with the sock weight of change
a fool's weapon
or a fortunate jangle of pocket-slung wealth

my father
dancing his hand
in dimes of distraction

someone counting out
the day
by the hen's worth

someone chumming the street
where poverty
scrambles for silver grain
like thirsting in new-fallen rain

if I am ever ungrateful
for the fat profile
of a small copper-faced man

or if I with
the cruel panjandrum
of a single bankable tyrant's jaw
and beard
some much-minted barbarian
seem disgruntled or am fraught by despair
or if it is my luck
to hold true
the fortunate currency of the heart
where I may be blessed by
the bent light
that suffers along the palm line
to the blue regions
of a better place than here

I am perhaps become a prism then
where every dolor
is always a counting house
and every coin
a micro measure
of a gathering backwards
both from sorrowful exaltation
and joyful sob

Writing the Darkness

I am
there beneath the black scrimshaw
of an overpainting where
the colour comes
at the brilliant reveal
bleeding through
the interstices of a blue scar
the brave
lightline of a luminous
vermillion or one
photosynthetic green vein
like the bent rib
of a living leaf's vivid lightning
this is I
the child amanuensis
of a compass point
in that secretarial knife slice
in that anthracitic scratch
of an unemprisoned hue
the millioning of night
as at one cold moon
a dog's eye weeps
and is blinded by time
old in the bones
like the wind limp
of a broken-branch orchard
the deracinate and desiccated arm
where the sapless
and thereby orphaned
ripening goes on
and is unattended
even as by the glorious rounding out

one sun-pure impregnation of seed-fat
mango glory hangs waiting
to be plucked
and succulent with rot
and a glutinous over-softening

this Cuban dog, the one we call Winky
scrofulous and lousy
flea-swollen
crimson and patchy
with relentless itch
curls down into unborn memory
seeking the sweet respite of sleep
that comes
only to the amniotic
startlement of a first spark
a sperm-pierced ovum
zygotic and then as with
the feral whelp
and a nascent milkening
hunger comes
in lactatory star-swirl to
this love-starved galaxy
where there is already suffering enough
for all

and my octogenarian mother
her mind
oversweetened by loss
dims down to one
sentence
"I am glad to be alive"

and a man I have known
imprisoned by a body
broken at birth
gives hope
the gift of his big attention
and makes me ashamed

no amount
of sinful expiation
in the world of woe
can stop
this jubilant pathos
of lice and tics or make him
refuse
the joyful urgency of tail-whipped appreciation
for meat scrap and
stale white inedible bread
folded over once
like the wincing of the field
what a winnowing
we will do
when with the ineluctable idiocy
of a single death
we fail
the sparrows
and do not hear their song
sewing the winter
with the warp and woof of insouciant white
and the interweaving
of a withering spring

The Truth of the Field

i

the spider
in the wine cellar
has woven
to the arched ceiling
of her dark cava, a web
fastened to the arc of brick
so it clings in wafts
like breath in the seven veils
of Salome

and she
inhabits the fog
of her home
lurking in the muslin loom
throbbing her thin legs
like a brief twitch
in fine filaments of plucked wire

she is a nearly invisible blur
from the full black bulb of her thorax
to the serrated thread of her forelegs
she is 'there'
in that grey tapestry of smoke
arachnid's ghost hovering
waiting, waiting   waiting
for the dying buzz
of hopeless wings

ii

the best wines of rarest vintage
age in morbid
shawls of blackened mould
their shapely bottle glass
draped in widow's weeds
rest layered in living rags
like the tossed-down tarnished gauze
of a brass cleaner

and in the earthy
fragrance
of closed-up houses
and linens too long
in the damp

this being
the pinot noir of 1949
the final memory
of the last labour
of the first vintner
the father
of this
truth of the field
this weather, this slope
this soil, these vines
this sun on the land
these grapes with one foot
in the shale
one summer, one season
one wine-maker's measure of rain

and the acrid flavour
of washed coin
to reward
the keeper for what
he has kept

iii

what thrives in each stone close
of cote d'or   lives on
as walled-up knowledge
for the cultivation
of a much-pampered plant
pruned to an exactitude
in height, planted
in a lovely symmetry
of perfect rows
placed there
with the precision of an ancient art

these hills and valleys
drink of the dreams
of Dionysus
and the sunken casks
of antiquity
breaking the surface
of the man-drowning sea

this thirst of first Caesar
this tainted breath
of the poet
who toasted Vercingetorix
dragged in chains through the streets of Rome

all of us forgetful
as the stone that says
our name

Lifeless—the rose of the heart

this stone I hold I have stolen
from the floor of the cave
Grotto Bernard
where the Maquis gathered
in hiding
to conspire against
the occupation of the Boche
during the last great war

it is drab granulated granite
rough to the touch
bullet-sized, amorphous
an archeological nothing
a dead eye
dropped from the slab face
of a dying escarpment
the ossified vitreous of demon rock

what it remembers
is, as with the memory
of all scree
—dirt, grime, earth
and the accidental gravity of footfall
the quickening
scramble of fear

what young man crawled here
like a broken-backed beast
the flesh of his bent knee
impregnate
with the sharp voice
of a mindless thing, stigmata

pierced in the palm, impressed
in the patella
that soft-skulled curved cap
of the necessary genuflection
not for worship
not for reverence of prayer
but there, humbled
in the dark spelunker's maw
where the cave
swallows hard
to take you in, along
with poor light
in the small-jawed
blackness of the entry point
you come there, arrive at
the low adit
and from there—depart
like the primordial mood
of water struck
from shale

what you know
of time and temporal
transformation
is all
emptying inward
like the pulled-through thread shadow
of the soul

at this grotto
you have heard

the old story
of betrayal and death

the unplanned
and unplannable
disconnection

between who you are
and who they were

lost and lingering
in what the wind says
of sunlight in summer
which is not
the green word
for breeze in a leaf

not lichen that
blackens the shale

nor the ferruginous red
of oxidized earth

but a breath
nonetheless
the last and unlasting
exhale

like the smoke
from the muzzle's blank O

that final and withering vowel
and the rose   upstruck

from the heart's
quick reply

The Hummingbird Moth
for M. Joubert

the weird moth
with the proboscis and forebody
of a hummingbird
and the quick flutter
of drab brown wings
comes to drink
the fragrant flower wells of lavender
like a tiny creature
from the book of beasts
beyond belief

and then, indoors
it dusts the windowpane
with a desperate
distempering inclarity
of blurring outward
it smudges
a frantic light and falls
as a damaged scrap
of torn
and glowering sky

the man who is speaking
here
bears the mark
on his forearm
of the number tattooed
at Auschwitz and Buchenwald

and he wells with tears
to tell us
how on Christmas Eve
the German guards
had placed a tannenbaum
in the parade square
of the concentration camp
its dark bowers blazing with candles

and they selected five prisoners
chosen at random
from the ranks
and brought them to a makeshift gallows
to be hung while the caught-men watched
is it cruel to die
as you die here
in summer
banging the window
with your tattering wings

the angels want out
where the truth
                wants in

and we weep the hear
them go still

this poem is dedicated to M. Pierre Joubert (b. 1927), who as a sixteen-year-old serving in the French resistance in the region Auxois de Bourgogne, was arrested by the Germans for his part in what was called "the Werner Affair" involving the death of a German Colonel. Joubert was sent to Auschwitz and then on to Buchenwald. He survived the war and returned to his home where he served for a time as Mayor of Villeverny where he still lives to this day.

Massingy-Les-Vitteaux, Burgundy, France
—Waddi Ram, Jordan
—Edinburgh Castle, Scotland

on our honeymoon
on the long green lawns
of Edinburgh castle
we sat together
in the soft light
of the Celtic gloaming
listening
to the military skirl of the pipes
in a grand tattoo
those twenty-five tartans
with the sporran
sweeping the knee
like the ghostly custodial
white of the great Hebrides
of old heaven
the battle cry
of a thousand-thousand
pibrochs brought to life
saying 'gainsay who dare'
when we were new
with our youth in us
like aromatic breath
of thistles and heather
and the uncommon purple
of bright desire
still in the wet
at the root of spring
with its
thrill in the source
of water's want

and the yet-to-be
fragrant mind
of a violet bloom
and then
we were near Wadi Ram
aging there, long-married tourists
in the desert heat
of Roman ruins

when two Arabs
in full Bedouin attire
seated together
in what remained
of the stone amphitheatre
of antiquity took up
their pipe and drum
and struck the dry torpor
of a strange song
'Scotland the Brave'
reminding me
of when el Laurence
was here
leading the fathers of the fathers
of the fathers of these Arab men
in war
against the Ottoman Turk
with the cry
"Akaba" as death on the wind
of empire

the weird duo
smiling for change
that spilled
from American palms
like the tossing
away of wishes for wells
and then only days later
alone in the village
Massingy-les-Vitteaux
the vice mayor
stopped us
full in the street

said, "may I play
for you?"
and he filled
the sheep gut
with twelve Burgundian breaths
so it swelled and he squeezed
and it droned in the breeze
where he played
the slave-master's song
"Amazing Grace"
and I thought
I too am a wretch
but for this

the loving grace
of a similar blue

same sun, same sky
same light on the land

with the dust
of one heart
brick red

*They Murdered Our Sons
While We Dreamed*

They Murdered Our Sons While We Dreamed

i

a beautiful star-blue Confederate battle flag
flies from the false wall
of a faux castle
fluttering among mock merlons and fake crenels
o'er-marking the house on the road
that runs north between Dover and Jarvis
what was once a symbol of the dying chivalry
of the doomed south
flaps there like strange laundry
drained of first meaning
as it is with the faded currency
of blockade runners
and those butternut ghosts
in slouch caps
loyal to old Virginia
loyal to Stonewall Jackson
loyal to General Lee
and all lost glory of fallen mansions
and the antebellum manners
of tobacco and cotton plantations
those burning acres
smoldering on the tongue of the land
like sunset gone crimson in smoke

ii

few who live now
know that during the American Civil War
Confederate agents
stationed in then-sympathetic Toronto
conspired to violence and piracy
against the hated Union
on Lake Erie

one particular man
wounded at Shenandoah
the veteran John Yates Baell
a discharged hero
made covert plans
to capture the Yankee ship
U.S.S. Michigan
and subsequent to that to use that ship to free
Confederate prisoners of war
held captive at Johnson's Island
in Sandusky Bay near Marblehead

he and his fellows
slipped in and out of Canada
like migratory waterfowl

first he boarded a small Sandusky steamer
the Philo Parsons
as a passenger taken on at Detroit
the steamer stopped
at Amherstburg
took on another group of men
when, near the island

Beall held a pistol to the helmsman's head
and seizing command of the ship by force
hoisted the stars & bars
put the crew ashore
and waited to take the Michigan

they were betrayed by an agent aboard the intended target
so the Michigan prepared for war
and they failed
when Beall's cabal refused the effort
out of fear
for they were few in number
and they fled

discouraged by the mutineers
he set a course for Canada
landed everyone ashore
and burned the Philo Parsons
to the waterline

iii

months later, captured boarding a train
in Niagara Falls
tried and convicted
as a spy
he was hanged
in the last winter of the war

iv

the gallows for his going
were of a new design
rather than taking the long drop
the tension of his dying
lifted him
from ground to sky
so he strangled upward
sprung from the earth
like flung cry of a startled gull
his last words before that being

"...absolute murder, brutal murder.
I die in defense and service
of my country."

V

legend suggests
his colleague and acquaintance
the actor John Wilkes Booth
assassinated the tyrant
Lincoln as an act of revenge
for this unjust execution

as it is
every elected Democrat had signed
a petition begging
presidential clemency

and Beall's mother
lamenting the fate of her doomed boy
said—"they murdered our sons
while we dreamed …"

vi

on every Friday the 13th
Port Dover
is haunted by the flap
and tatter
of a thousand insignificant banners
fluttering away
with the torn and wounded colours
of the secessionist south

these pretending rebels
wend their way
through town
passing under the clock tower
marking the wrong hour
with the lake in their mirror
they stop
to lean the hot tick
of their cooling engines
at a cant near Powell Park
the shining teardrop chrome
with its redolence of gasoline
reflecting a blur of blue sky
as they dismount
and walk away
into the slow forgetting
future
that eventually
forgets us all

vii

and though this has nothing whatsoever to do
with the death of John Yates Beall

yet
in the smoky fragrance
of those end-of-week streets

in the roar of engines
that trail their fumes

and in the battlefield backfire
of their coming in and going hence

I hear something of the *nothing* that is there

To a Fiend (owning my juvenilia) and beyond ...

Even at the Worst of Times

Even at the worst of times, writing poems has been joyous and rewarding.
Al Purdy "To See the Shore"

(The very first poems I ever wrote, when I began thinking I might some day become a poet, were bad in every sense of the word but one — I did not know how bad they were. They were bad beyond the know of bad. But they were always a pleasure to write. And that pleasure in writing remains with me even to this day. Whenever I am writing I am chasing the feeling I feel arising from the thrill of writing when the writing is going well.)

This opening paragraph taken from my essay "Even at the Worst of Times," appearing in the anthology *And Left a Place to Stand On: Poems and Essays on Al Purdy (Hidden Brook Press, 2009)* expresses a sentiment that remains true to my feelings concerning my work even as I compose this afterward to *This is How We See the World: the chapbook years.* The book begins with "Poem for One or More Feet," a book which I wrote as a third-year student of English at University of Western Ontario in London, and culminates in "They Murdered Our Sons While We Dreamed," along with the complete content of fourteen chapbooks in between for a total of sixteen chapbooks published between 1973 and 2016.

*

In June of 1960 little eight-year-old schoolboy Johnny Lee composed his first poem. The teacher had decided that we should make a Father's Day Card for our dads. She wrote several verses on the blackboard from which we were expected to choose. Apparently I did not like the examples she gave, so I decided to make up my own. I didn't exactly understand the nature of a Father's Day Card, though I did have a notion of what sounded like greeting-card language. I came up with what I thought to be a suitable phrase. I wrote the title for my greeting on the outside of the card. What I had meant to write was "To a Friend," but I was a careless lad and I elided the 'r' from the word so the title of my Father's Day Card became *"To a Fiend!"* On the inside of the card I drew a television set which I coloured brown of body, green of screen, and to the interior I taped a single hexagonal Canadian nickel. The formal card constructed of twice folded typing paper flopped with the weight of the coin and the scotch tape lost its stickiness and stained the page over time. My father cherished that card and would often take it out and show it to gales of laughter and deep guffaws in his own basso-profundo farmer's voice. He loved that card. After all, I was his son and he was my own best fiend. My best fiend forever.

**

I did not write another poem until the morning after the night the Beatles first appeared on Ed Sullivan on Sunday, February 9, 1964. In fact, between the ages of eight and twelve I had come to hate poetry because our only experience with poetry as school children involved memory work. I begrudgingly memorized poems like Bliss Carmen's "The Ships of Yule," Robert Frost's "Stopping by Woods on a Snowy Evening," and "The Duel," by Eugene Field.

That last poem began:
THE GINGHAM *dog and the calico cat*
Side by side on the table sat;
'T was half-past twelve, and (what do you think!)
Nor one nor t' other had slept a wink!

And I remember struggling to commit those lines to memory for the purpose of oratory regurgitation in school. The following day I stood rather stiff and formal, with my body quaking, my hands trembling, my knees knocking, my voice quivering, my mind blanking, my heart beating like the ten count of a sugar-hungry horse and I hated every minute. I loathed that damned calico dog even more than I despised Bliss Carman's gallant barkentine or Robert Frost's winter miles. Sometimes we were required to write out the poems the teacher had selected, it seemed as weapons of torture. Then we were marked on our ability to duplicate not only word for word exactness, but also spelling and punctuation. This is the tale of woe concerning how the bouncing baby boy who loved Mother Goose's "Baa Baa black sheep," and the rhapsodic "Dinner Time," my Dad's personal favourite that began "Tuggin' at the bottle,/ An' it's O, you're mighty sweet!" came if ever so briefly to hate poetry.

Then the Beatles woke me up! They kindled the desire to write. I began writing in earnest for two reasons. I wanted Paul McCartney's attention, and I craved my father's approval. The very first poems I wrote were a series of awful verses in praise of the Beatles. I had seen a few poems published in a farm newspaper. One verse by Miss Rhoda Marrison of Nova Scotia began, "Ringo, named for all his rings/ Everyone listens when he sings." A limerick by Barbie of Prince George, B.C. went "Paul McCartney is cutest of the Beatles/ For him I would sit upon needles:" and lastly Mary Ann Frykas of Gilbert Plains, Manitoba wrote "England's Beatles are real cool,/ They all come from Liverpool." I thought to myself, *I could write poems like those*, and they might even be published, and if they appear in print, maybe one of the Beatles might read them — and then my life would be complete. This is how I thought as a twelve-year-old farm boy. I immediately set myself the task of writing not just one poem, but a whole suite of poems inspired by and dedicated to The Beatles.

***

My first published poem appeared in my Ridgetown high-school yearbook in 1970. That poem has not reappeared in print in any form since then. Though not a shameful first effort, it is not particularly strong. It is a piece of juvenilia that is not so very awful as to make me ashamed, and not of sufficient merit to appear anywhere but here in very italicized context with this caveat: *'please forgive me, I was only sixteen when I wrote these words.'*

Thoughts of a Mouse at High Tide

Should I submerge my eyes
beneath the frothy
to and fro
of suicide?
Lay on my side
beneath the foam of surf
that licks the bay.
I may fill you
and refill you
like a happy sailor
tumbling through his pay
though when all is lost
I shall go back for more
yet there is
no other chance
to fork the change
from empty pockets
of forgotten dream.
I will leave you now
wasted water
and tremble through
the backwash of the flood
with nothing to do
but to begin
at the end

There's another poem, written at around the same time that I actually stand behind. I think it's not bad for a seventeen-year-old school boy.

My Alibi for an Eventful Wednesday in May

I am lost in a room
where we did not meet
listening to the song
that isn't ours
thinking the thoughts
I didn't think
when we didn't meet here.
I don't remember
what you didn't wear then.
I think
it wasn't pink.
I don't recall
what you didn't
whisper in my ear.
I think it wasn't spring
when we weren't here.
I don't remember
not seeing the carriage
that didn't bring us here.
I don't remember
not kissing you
after we didn't drink
champagne.
All that I recall
is that the nude
who didn't dance
on the table
wasn't you.

Not that it matters much beyond the fact of it being a curiosity, but I remember writing that poem in the library between classes at RDHS. When it became necessary for me to remove my possessions from the family farm prior to the sale of the land, I found the original handwritten copy of that poem composed in a cursive I barely recognize as being that of my own hand. The poem is composed in blue-ink ballpoint pen on lined three-hole notebook paper torn from a binder. I discovered it in a box along with love letters written to an old girlfriend Cathy Jeanne Morden during my second summer home from university.

The next poems I had published were printed in the *Gazette,* a biweekly student newspaper. A local poet named Jamie Hamilton edited a feature called 'The Bull Ring,' and the editors of the newspaper also showcased poems in the centre of the paper on a page called "Page Five" with a photograph complimenting the selected pieces of writing. My poems appeared frequently in both the Bull Ring and on Page Five. In third year, Governor General Award winning poet Margaret Avison was appointed Writer in Residence. I worked up the courage to go to her and show her my work. I left her a manuscript I'd called *The Madrigal's Revenge.* She praised the title and told me she'd read the poems and that I should come back in a week or so and she'd give me her response. Since I am quite shy by nature, I hadn't gone to visit her until after Christmas, and I returned to her office in February, the day after Groundhog Day, just before reading week. She opened her door, motioned me to a chair, sat across from me with my manuscript on her lap, smiled at me, inhaled – exhaled – inhaled – exhaled, saying nothing at all. I had no idea what to think. Then she handed me a poem she had composed for me.

<u>To John Lee</u> (Groundhog Day 1973)

    your speech (spit teeth   ah flow of breath)
    grass tussock place   swimskin
    eyeblink   eyelash
    illumined   glimmering
    tongue touch tip tremble
    and simple surge
           breaks open
                breaks.

Seals
    shapes
new ocean ledges
new fur slick   wildly shy
rump gentle   humped up silent
moon milled   mindcombed
wind yelling   all night out there
strongholds.
          The open stronghold
              breaks open

                          open

    to sun and sea sweat
    sweetgrass evening hours
    and the inwash of all dark
        floods to single out
            the fragile poet fierce in
                song and sinew

Hear how in his voice he **makes a break** in hollowing
                        wholeness   **jubilant**

                              Margaret Avison

She praised my work highly and encouraged me with some enthusiasm. I didn't know it at the time, but she had been reading my poems to members of the English Department soliciting kindred admiration. I had five poems and one short story published in the English Department's journal *The Pom Seed*, and she kindly composed a letter of recommendation on my behalf suggesting that Coach House Press in Toronto might give consideration to a manuscript of mine. I sent my first effort to them. It was called *Poem for One or More Feet,* and almost immediately I received a letter of acceptance from Victor Coleman. A year later, a knock came at my door and McLean Jameson of Applegarth Follies, a literary publisher living in London appeared on the step requesting a manuscript. That too was accepted and it became my first book *Poems Only a Dog Could Love*. Due to circumstances too complicated to relate herein, the Coach House book would never appear. When it came to Applegarth Follies attention that that book would not appear, Jameson committed his press to publishing that book as well. Unfortunately, Applegarth Follies folded up shop before *Poem for One or More Feet* appeared, though it was completely type set and ready to go. So there I was, not yet twenty-one years of age, and already I had had several manuscripts accepted for publication. Thus began a life of good fortune. Although I've suffered a few setbacks, mine has been a lucky life. The book you hold began with that short series *Poem for One of More Feet* which first appeared in print in my second collection *Love Among the Tombstones*.

****

In conclusion I'll provide a brief description of each subsequent chapbook.

To Kill a White Dog

This short connected poem was inspired by a story I heard while traveling on the Grand River Belle. The opening lines of the poem came to me after hearing Francis Sparshott reading from his long poem "The Cave of Trophonius," and it was first published by Brick Books.

The Day Jane Fonda Came to Guelph

The publisher of a journal called *The Plowman* had accepted several of my poems so when he solicited a chapbook, I sent him the poems that would appear under this title. To my great surprise, he immediately accepted the poems. I engaged the services of my friend, the visual artist Frank Woodcock, who produced a cover image involving Jane Fonda's reflection in a rear-view mirror as she drove her car into the city of Guelph. She had come there to film the movie *Agnes of God*. I was delighted by the rapidity with which the chapbook appeared on my doorstep, though I confess that I was startled and not just a little disappointed by the fact that my typescript had simply been photocopied on cheap paper.

The Echo of Your Words Has Reached Me

In early July of 1996, I flew to Baffin Island with my elder son Dylan and along with two others we walked the Weasel River trail crossing the Arctic Circle camping along the way. We spent two weeks walking and I wrote a series of poems that culminated in this chapbook published by Mekler & Deahl. I received the Order of Arctic Adventurers in recognition for my trek. Global Television featured the opening poem "I Too Can Show the Way," in collaboration with McLean's Magazine in a program called "Canadian Heroes."

An Almost Silent Drumming

In the summer of 2000 my wife and I flew to Johannesburg, South Africa where I was a guest lecturer/poet at Witwatersrand University English Department. While we were there we traveled in Soweto and spent a week living in a chalet on the outskirts of a game reserve and going on a photography safari. I wrote most of these poems sitting poolside in suburban Johannesburg. After the book was published I received letters of praise from both Nelson Mandela and Desmond Tutu for my poems. This chapbook received recognition in three chapbook awards, one as a manuscript and two post-publication Honourable mentions.

The Mission of Angels

This poem is the title poem of a longer manuscript comprised of the following two chapbooks. I won Honourable Mention in the Bliss Carmen Poet Laureate Award for this manuscript.

In a Language with No Word for Horses

I divided the aforementioned manuscript into two parts, this first part representing the poems inspired by Samuel de Champlain's travels to New France.

Though Their Joined Hearts Drummed Like Larks

This suite of poems focuses on the travels of Champlain's companion Étienne Brûlé who was the first European to visit much of what is now southwestern Ontario. Though he was a young man in his late teens at the time, due to the fact that Brûlé had a facility for languages he was sent by Champlain to live among the native people of the region, to learn their customs and their language.

Eventually he would betray Champlain and fall victim to a fate similar to that of Jesuit missionary Brébeuf.

Bright Red Apples of the Dead

On his deathbed my father made a simple request, "I just want one red apple." Although he did not know it at the time, a bright red apple is often a symbol of death or dying. These poems were written at the time of his passing or shortly thereafter and they represent homage to my father.

Thirty-Three-Thousand Shades of Green

On September 11, 2001 I was teaching Sport Literature at Western University. I first heard the awful news concerning the attack on the twin towers and the pentagon listening to the radio in the early afternoon several hours after the two events. In October I traveled to Stephen's Point Wisconsin where I was a guest of American poet Dale Ritterbusch, a professor of English literature seconded to the air force academy where he taught officer candidates. This series of poems are inspired by my response to events of one fateful day in the late summer of 2001 and the coalition's invasion that followed. To my mind warfare is always a failure of the human imagination and these poems partake in the hope for peace and harmony in a troubled world.

But Where Were the Horses of Evening

As a frequent visitor to the Trappist monastery Abbey of Gethsemani near Bardstown, Kentucky, I have always found the monastery and the surrounding region to be very inspiring. These poems were all written over the course of several visits to the monastery. I often traveled in the company of Canadian poets and most frequently visited the monastery with my close friend Marty Gervais. Over the course of time I have become friends with Trappist monk Brother Paul Quenon and professor Robert (Bob) Hill, both of whom are fine poets in their own rite.

Let Light Try All the Doors

This manuscript was selected for the distinction of having won the Rubicon Chapbook Award in 2009. The poems were inspired by my first trip to Korea, the year my elder son Dylan was married there and by a visit to Thailand where my wife Cathy and I accompanied my son and his bride on their honeymoon.

One Leaf in the Breath of the World

Winner of the inaugural Golden Grassroots Chapbook Award, the poems in this suite are mostly inspired by life in the landscape of home.

Adoration of the Unnecessary

This series of poems mostly inspired by living in our lake house overlooking Long Point Bay on Lake Erie in Port Dover won First Honourable Mention in the Golden Grassroots Chapbook Award for 2015.

This is How We See the World

These poems were written while we were traveling in Peru in the spring of 2015. The poem "Lalo's Walls," won the Hour Glass Poetry Award in 2016, one thousand dollar prize for best poem.

Counting Cranes

This series of poems won First Honourable Mention in the 2016 Cranberry Tree Press Chapbook Award and the poem "Climbing the Great Wall of China" won first place in the Literary Encyclopedia Award.

Traveling Through Each Other's Lives

The poems in this section of the book were written while I was traveling in France and in Cuba.

They Murdered Our Sons While We Dreamed

This long poem was first featured in video form at the Harbour Museum in Port Dover. The poem inspired in part by the story of John Yates Beahl (pronounced Bell) executed as a spy during the American Civil War for his activities on Lake Erie. His story is conflated with the Friday the Thirteenth celebrations taking place every Friday the Thirteenth in Port Dover when the town where I live is visited by motorcycles from all over North America.

Bio Notes about the Author:

In 2005 John B. Lee was inducted as Poet Laureate of Brantford in perpetuity. The same year he received the distinction of being named Honourary Life Member of The Canadian Poetry Association and The Ontario Poetry Society. In 2007 he was made a member of the Chancellor's Circle of the President's Club of McMaster University and named first recipient of the Souwesto Award for his contribution to literature in his home region of southwestern Ontario and he was named winner of the inaugural Black Moss Press *Souwesto Award* for his contribution to the ethos of writing in Southwestern Ontario. In 2011 he was appointed Poet Laureate of Norfolk County (2011-14) and in 2015 Honourary Poet Laureate of Norfolk County for life. A recipient of over eighty prestigious international awards for his writing he is winner of the $10,000 CBC Literary Award for Poetry, the only two time recipient of the People's Poetry Award, and 2006 winner of the inaugural Souwesto Orison Writing Award (University of Windsor). In 2007 he was named winner of the Winston Collins Award for Best Canadian Poem, an award he won again in 2012. In 2016 he won Honourable Mention in the Cranberry Tree Press Chapbook Award and the Golden Grassroots Press Award, Honourable Mention in the Drummond Poetry Award, First Place in the Scugog Poetry Award, First place in the Hour Glass Poetry Award, First Place in the Literary Encyclopedia Award, and Honourable Mention in the Peace Poetry Award. He has well-over seventy books published to date and is the editor of seven anthologies including two best-selling works: *That Sign of Perfection*: poems and stories on the game of hockey; and *Smaller Than God*: words of spiritual longing. He co-edited a special issue of *Windsor Review—Alice Munro: A Souwesto Celebration* published in the fall of 2014. His work has appeared internationally in over 500 publications, and has been translated into French, Spanish, Korean and Chinese. He has read his work in nations all over the world including South Africa, France, Korea, Cuba, Canada and the United States. He has received letters of praise from Nelson Mandela, Desmond Tutu, Australian Poet Les Murray, and Senator Romeo Dallaire. Called "the greatest living poet in English," by poet George Whipple, he lives in Port Dover, Ontario where he works as a full time author.

Other Hidden Brook Press books by John B. Lee.
www.HiddenBrookPress.com

Island on the Wind-Breathed Edge of the Sea
ISBN – 978-1-897475-19-5

In the Muddy Shoes of Morning
ISBN 978-1-897475-64-5

In This We Hear The Light
ISBN – 978-1-897475-96-6

Window Fishing
The night we caught Beatlemania – 3rd Edition
ISBN – 978-1-927725-14-6

Sweet Cuba
The Building of a Poetic Tradition: 1608-1958
Translators: John B. Lee, Dr. Manuel de Jesús Velázquez León
ISBN 978-1-897475-53-9

For a full description
you can find any of these fine books
on Amazine.

OR

you can order
from any local bookstore.

www.ingramcontent.com/pod-product-compliance
Lightning Source LLC
LaVergne TN
LVHW040035080526
838202LV00045B/3342